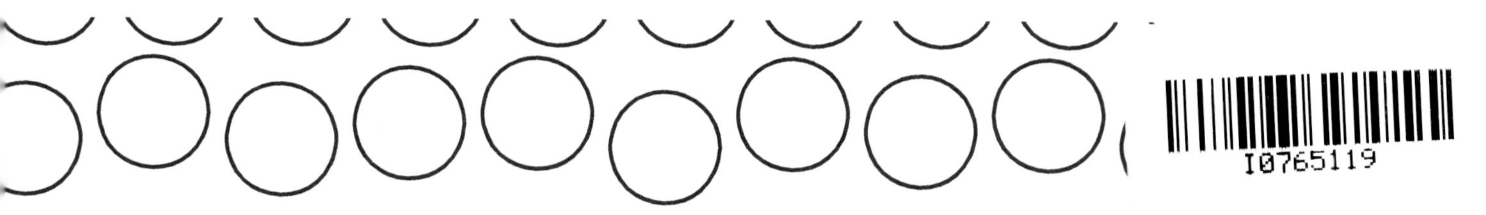

CHRISTMAS MERMAID

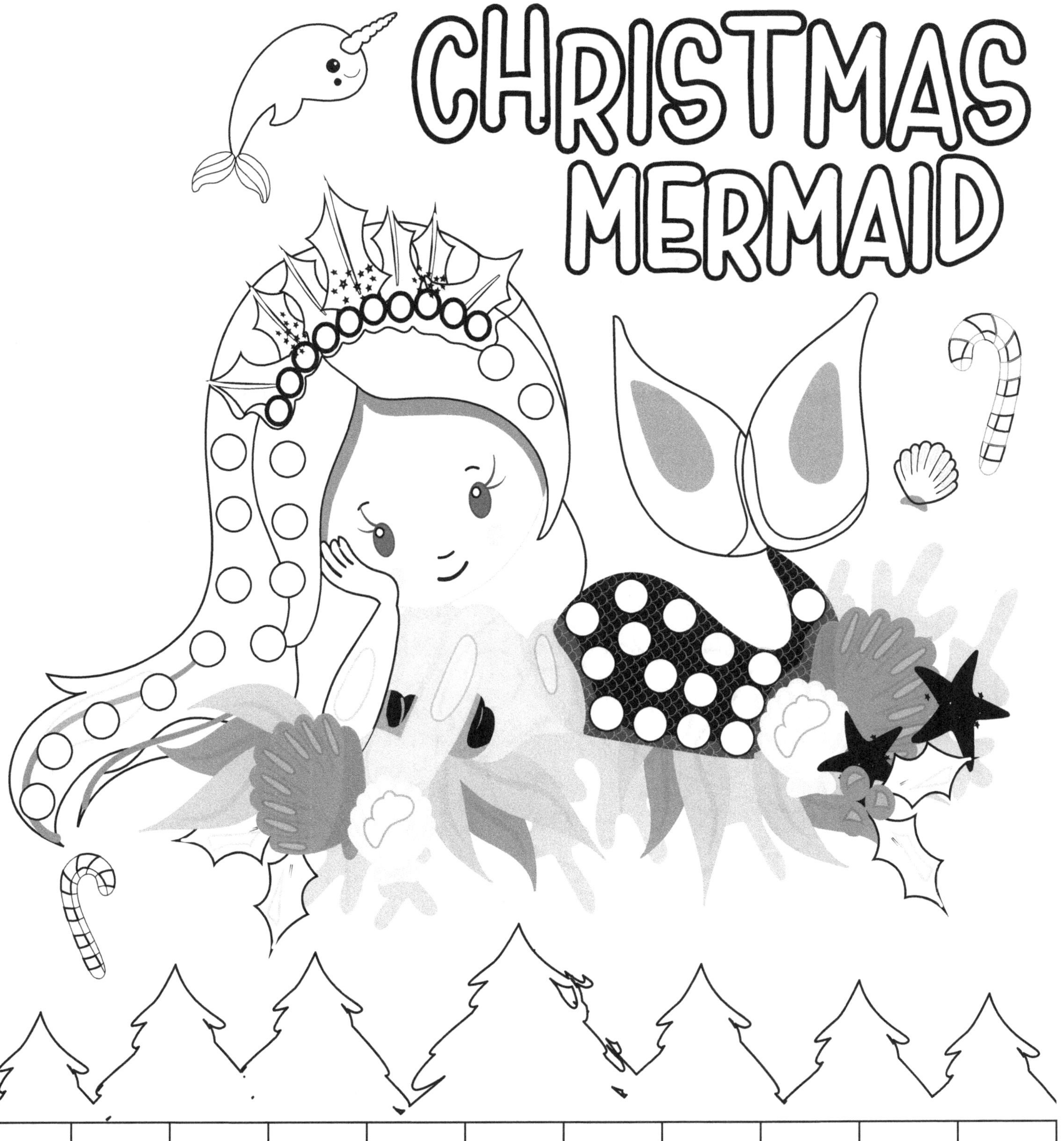

This Book Belongs To

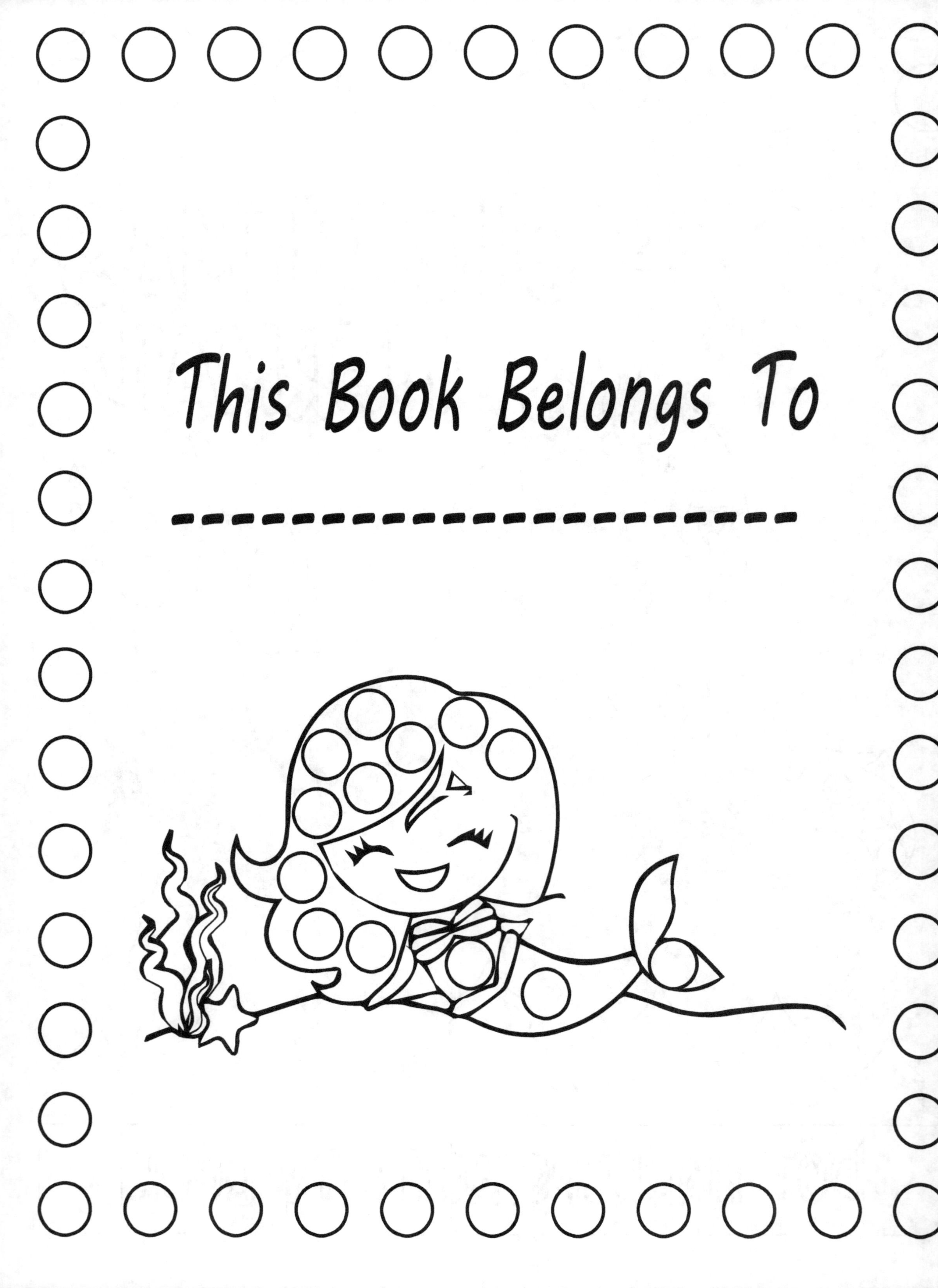

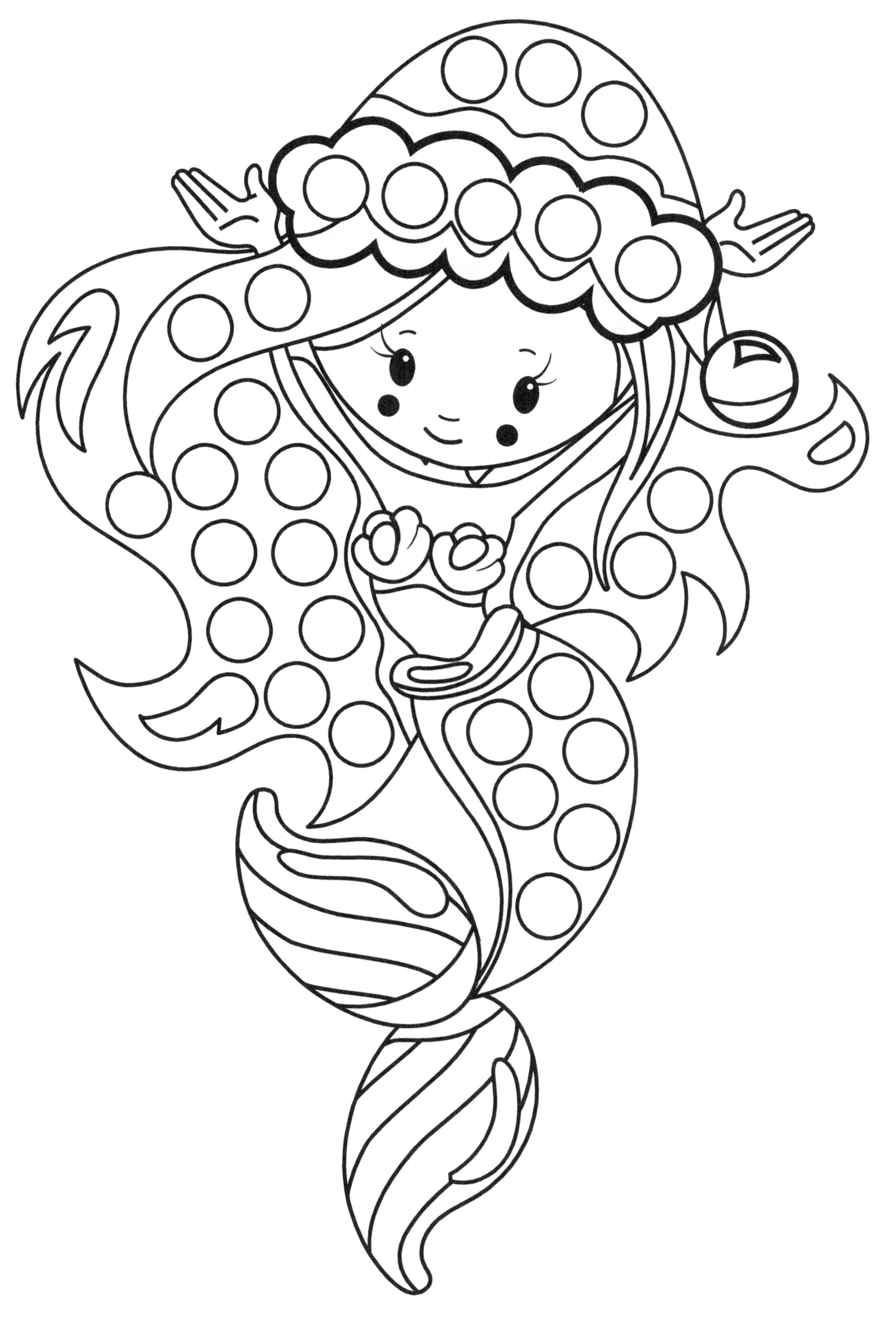

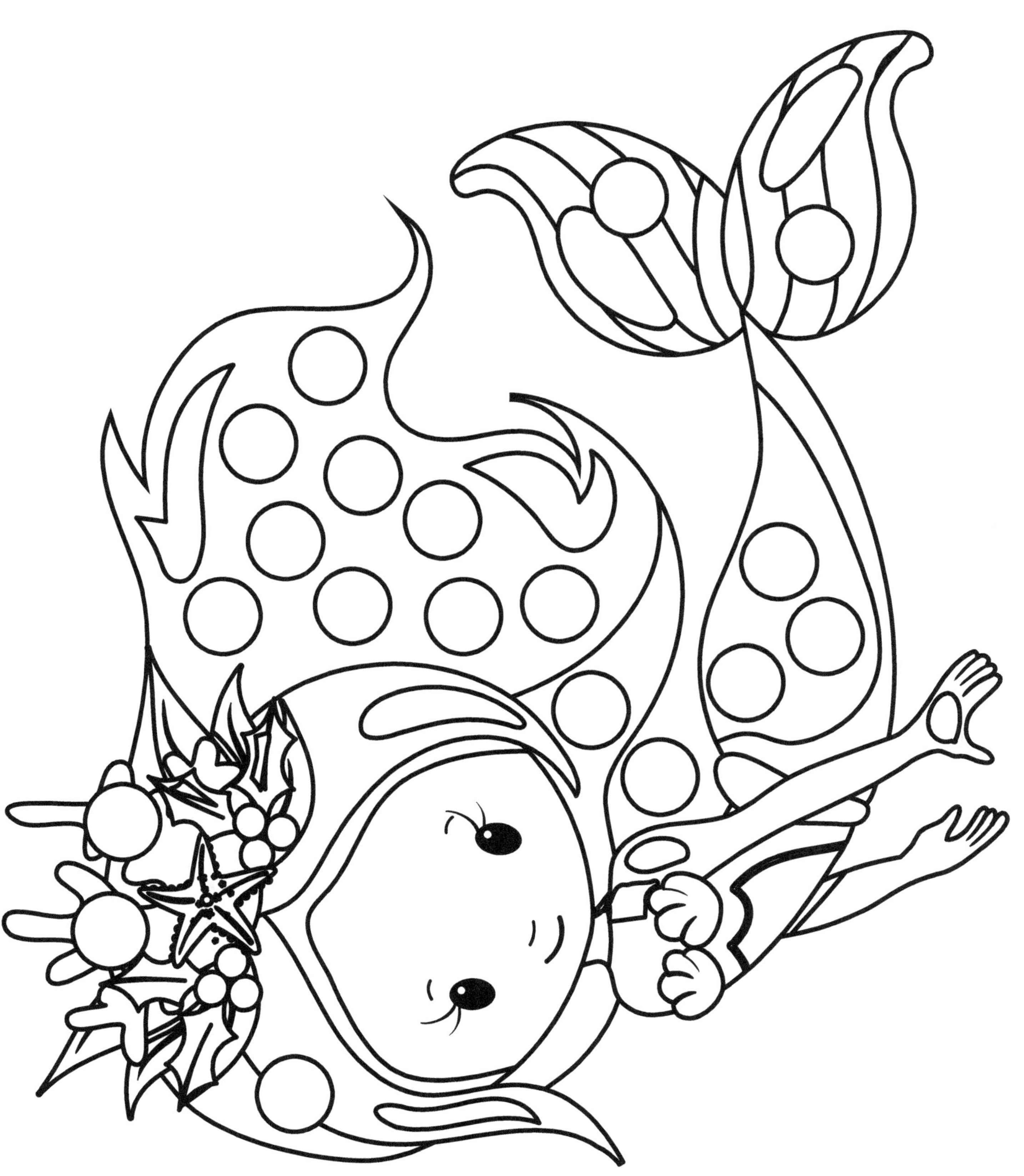

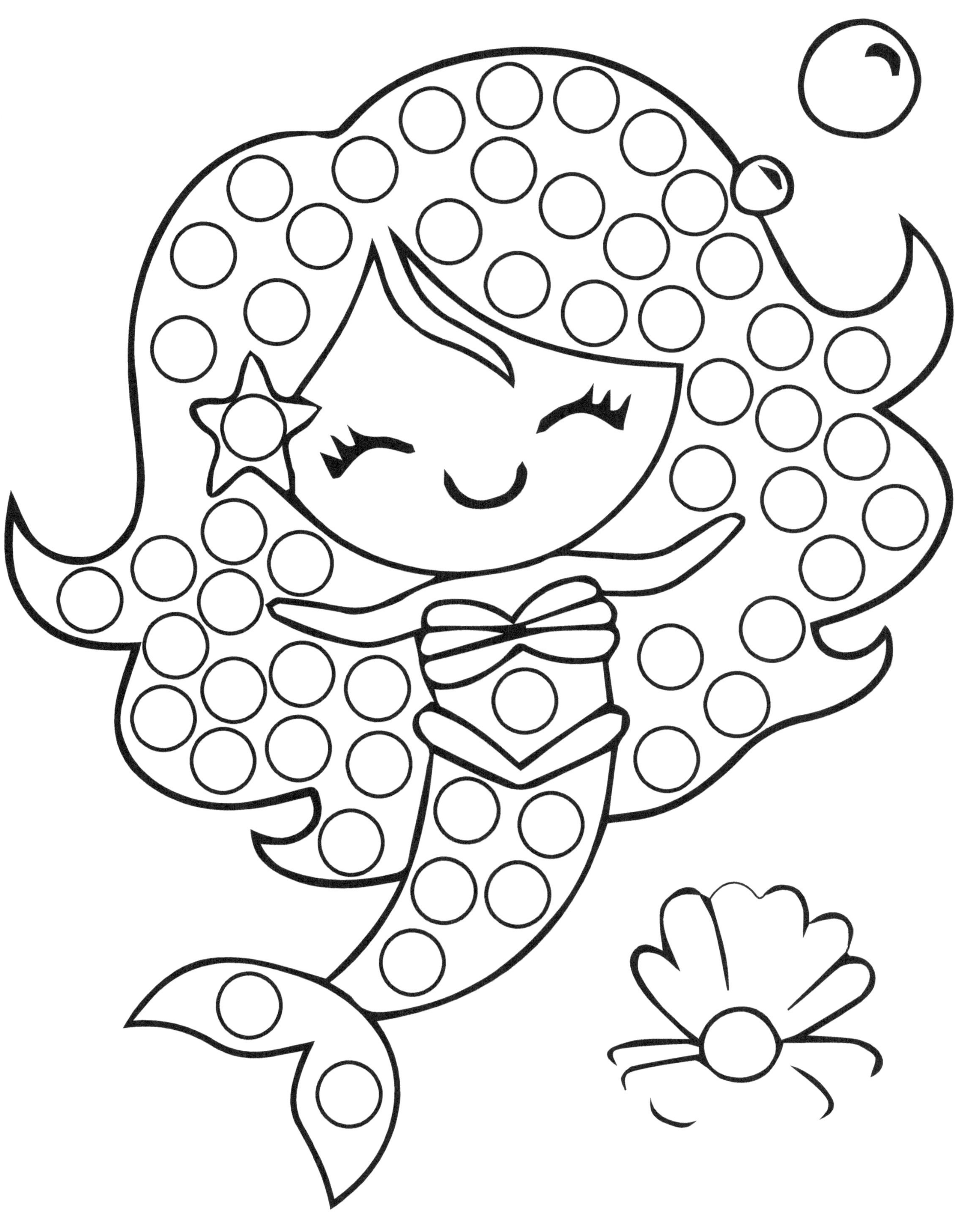

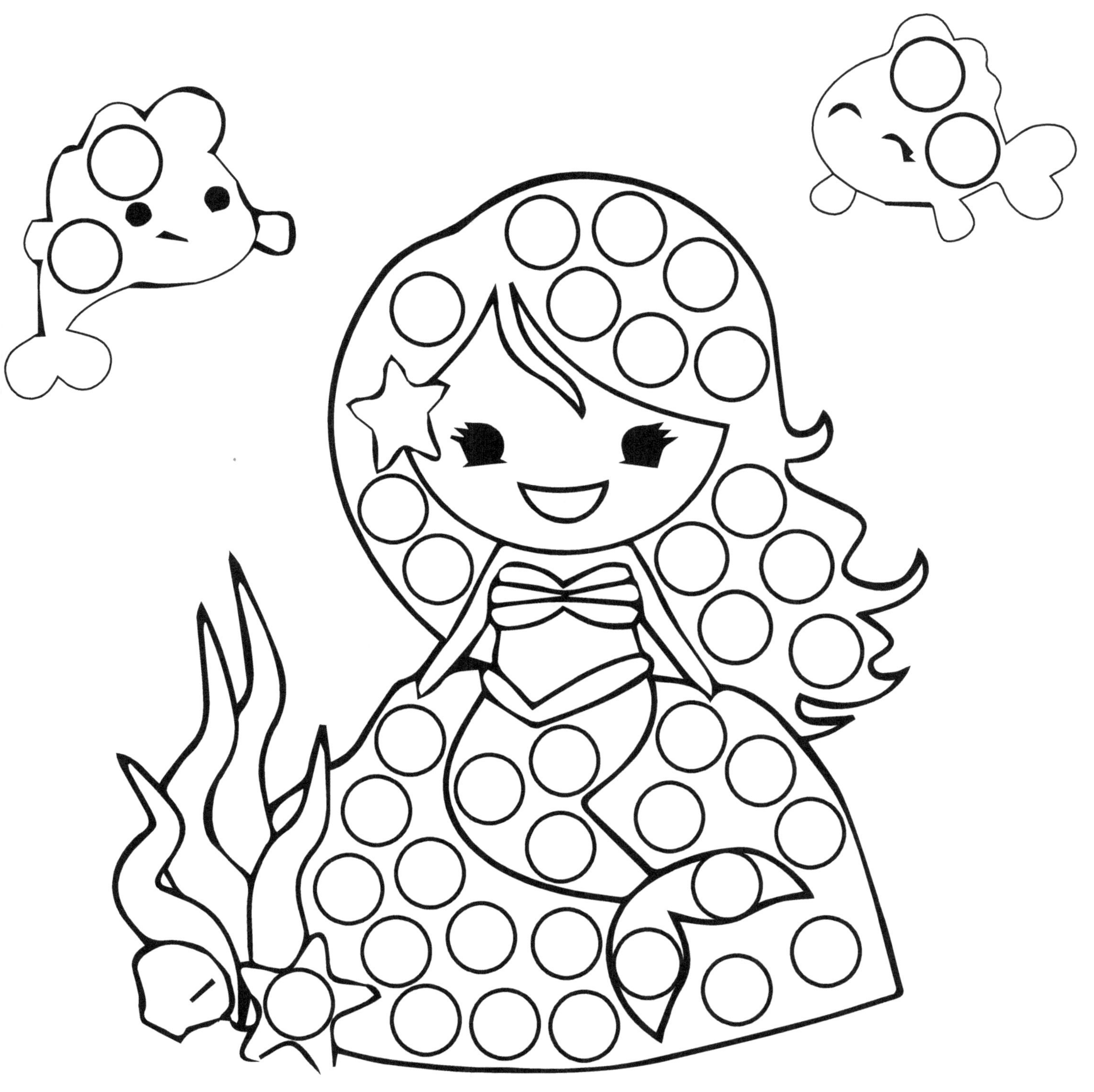

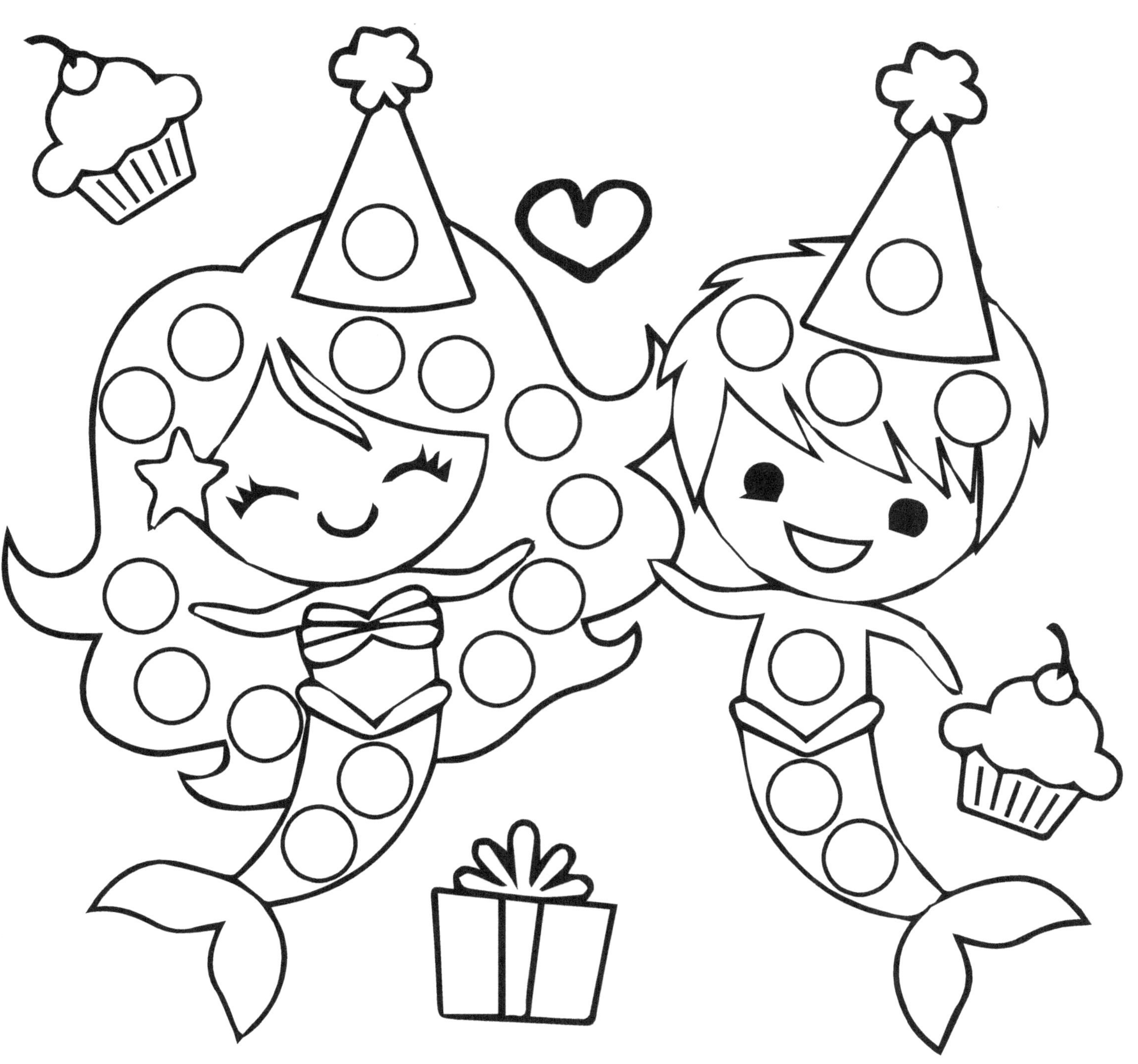

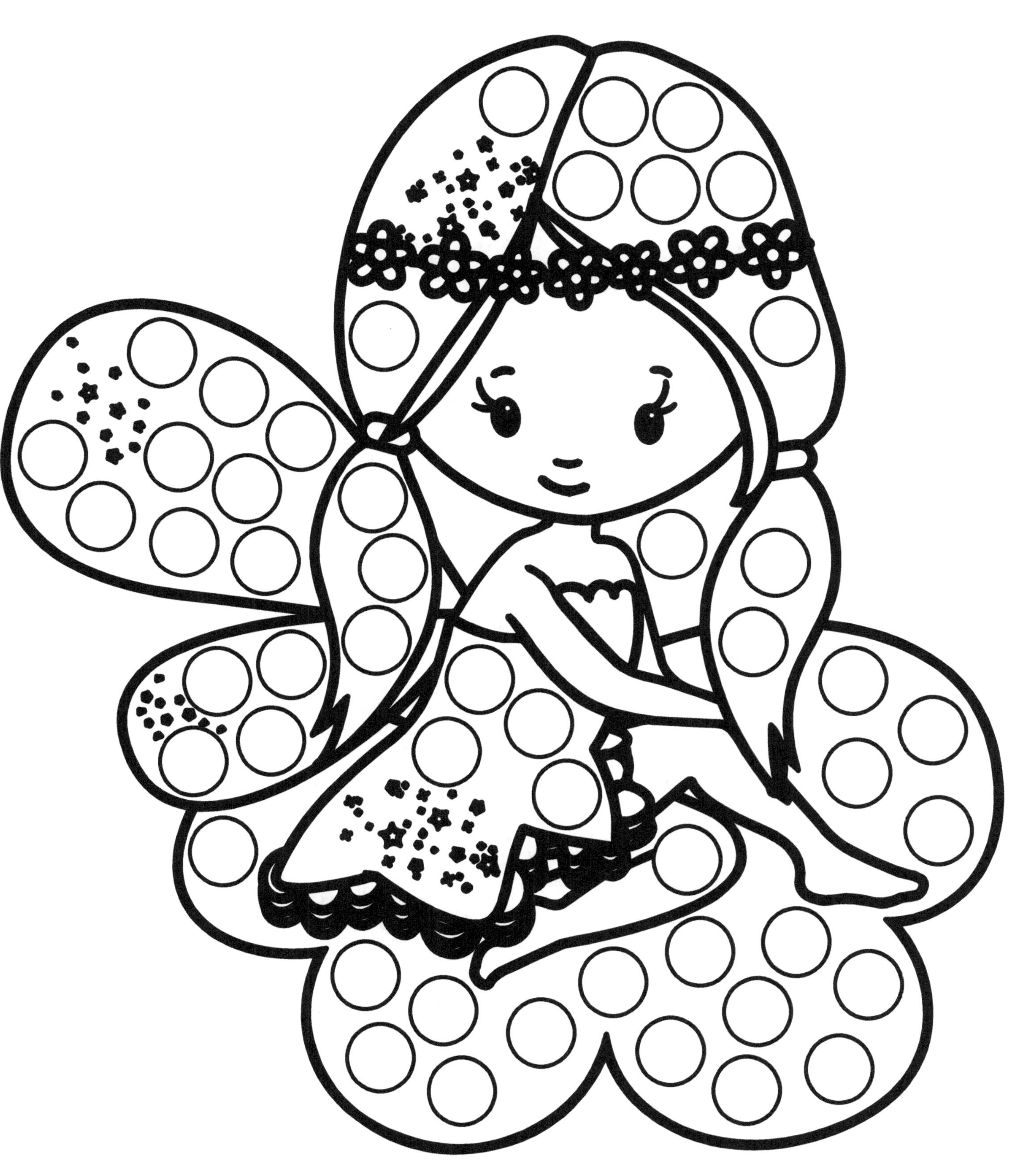

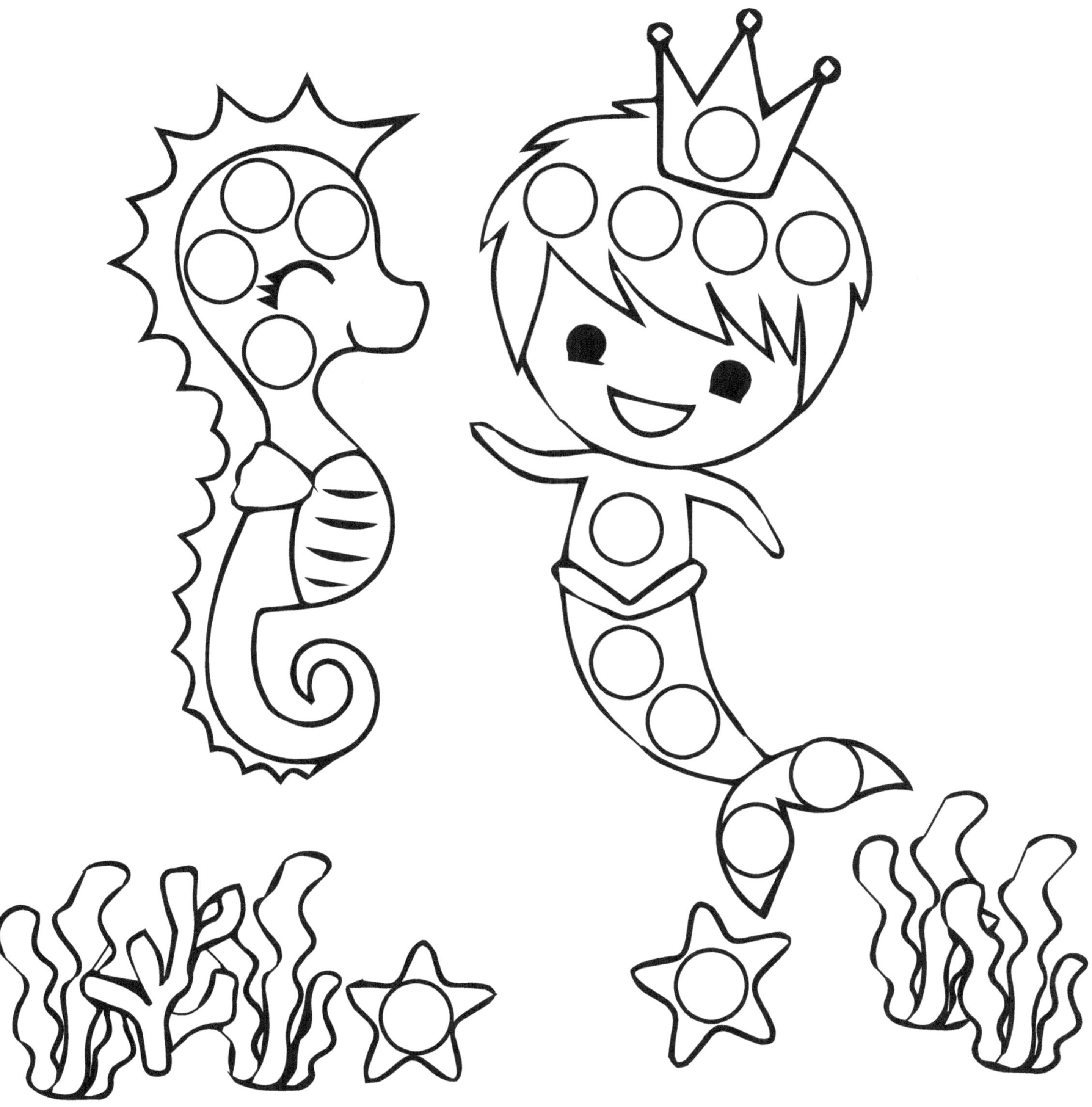

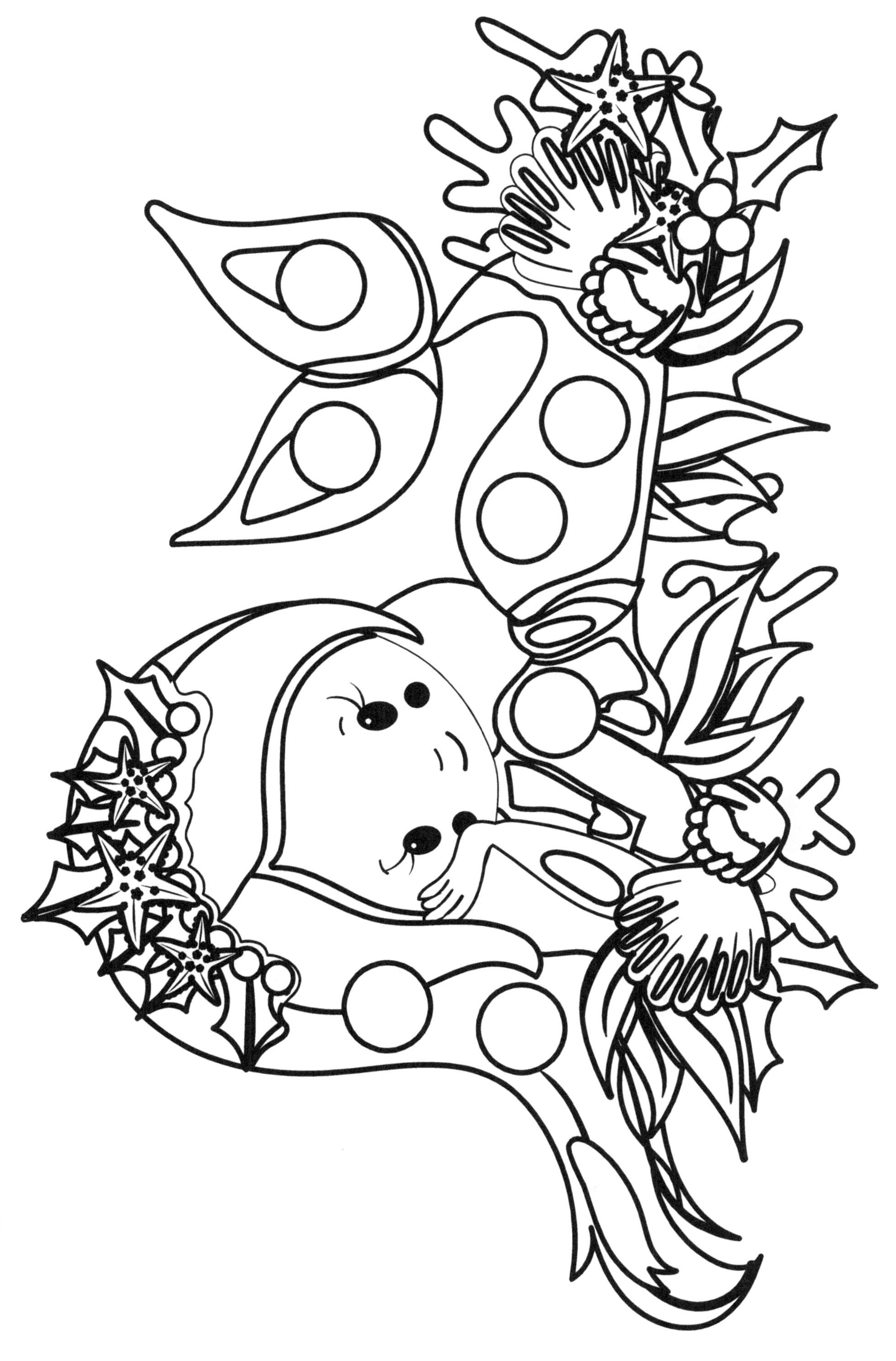

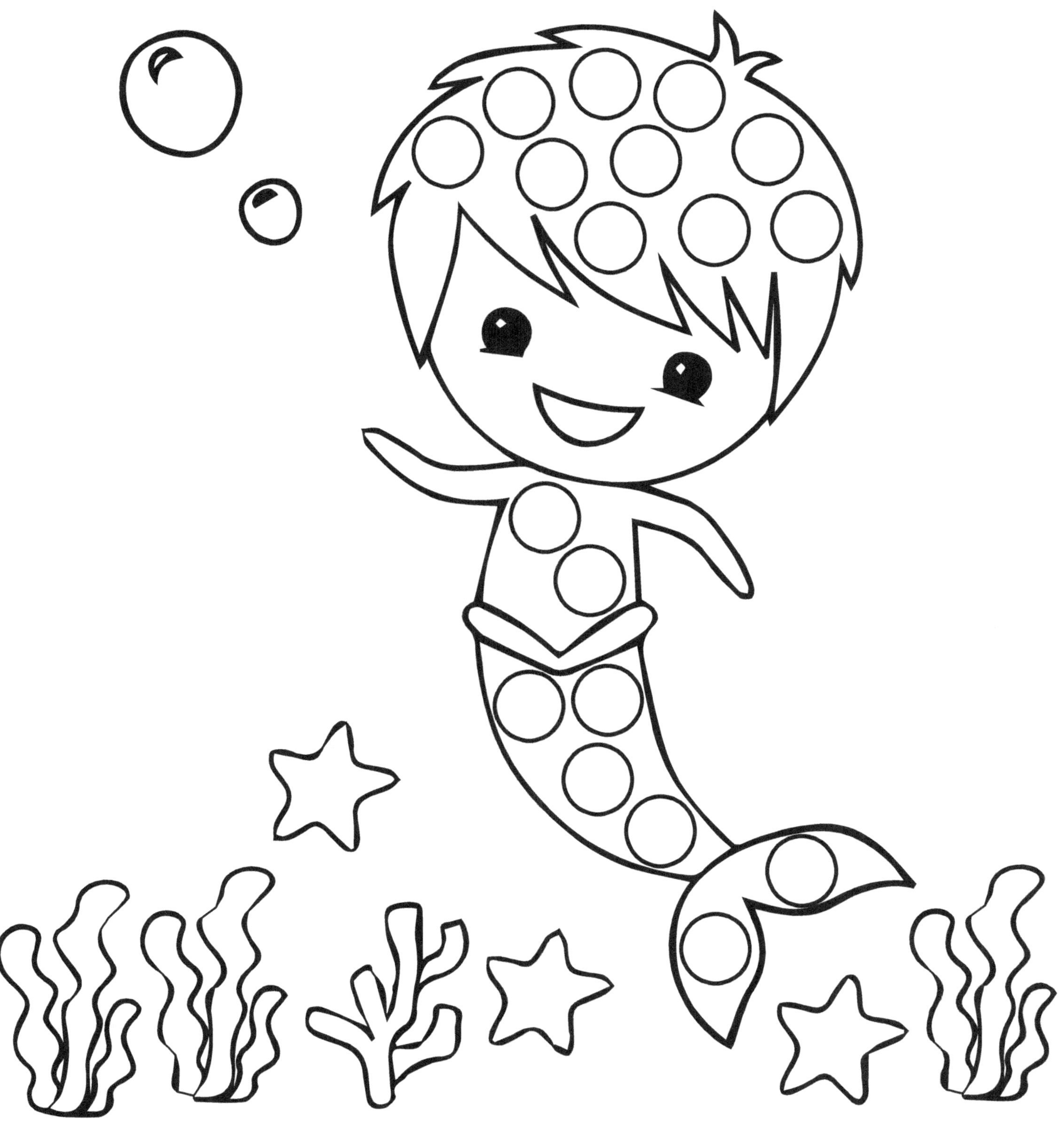

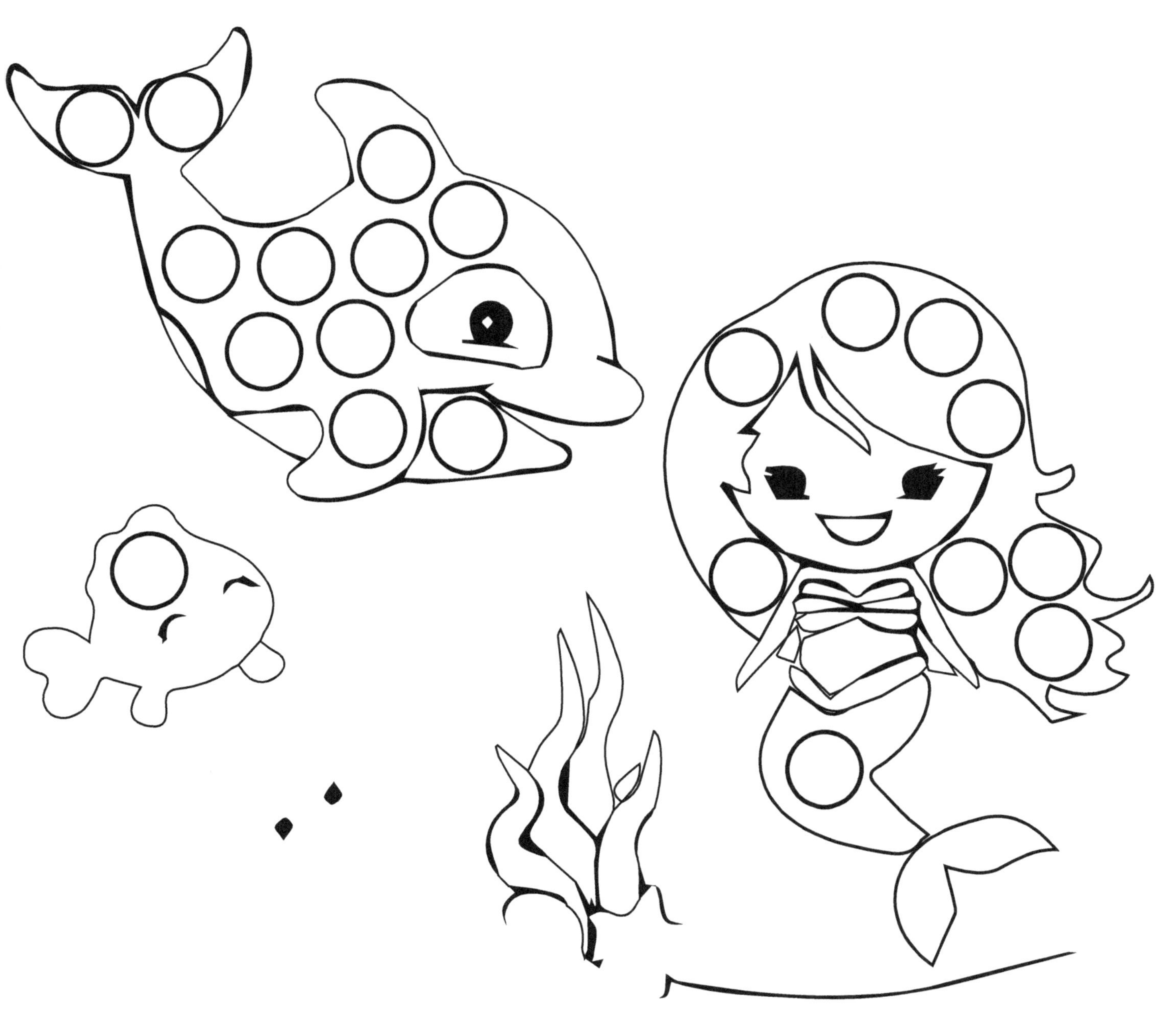

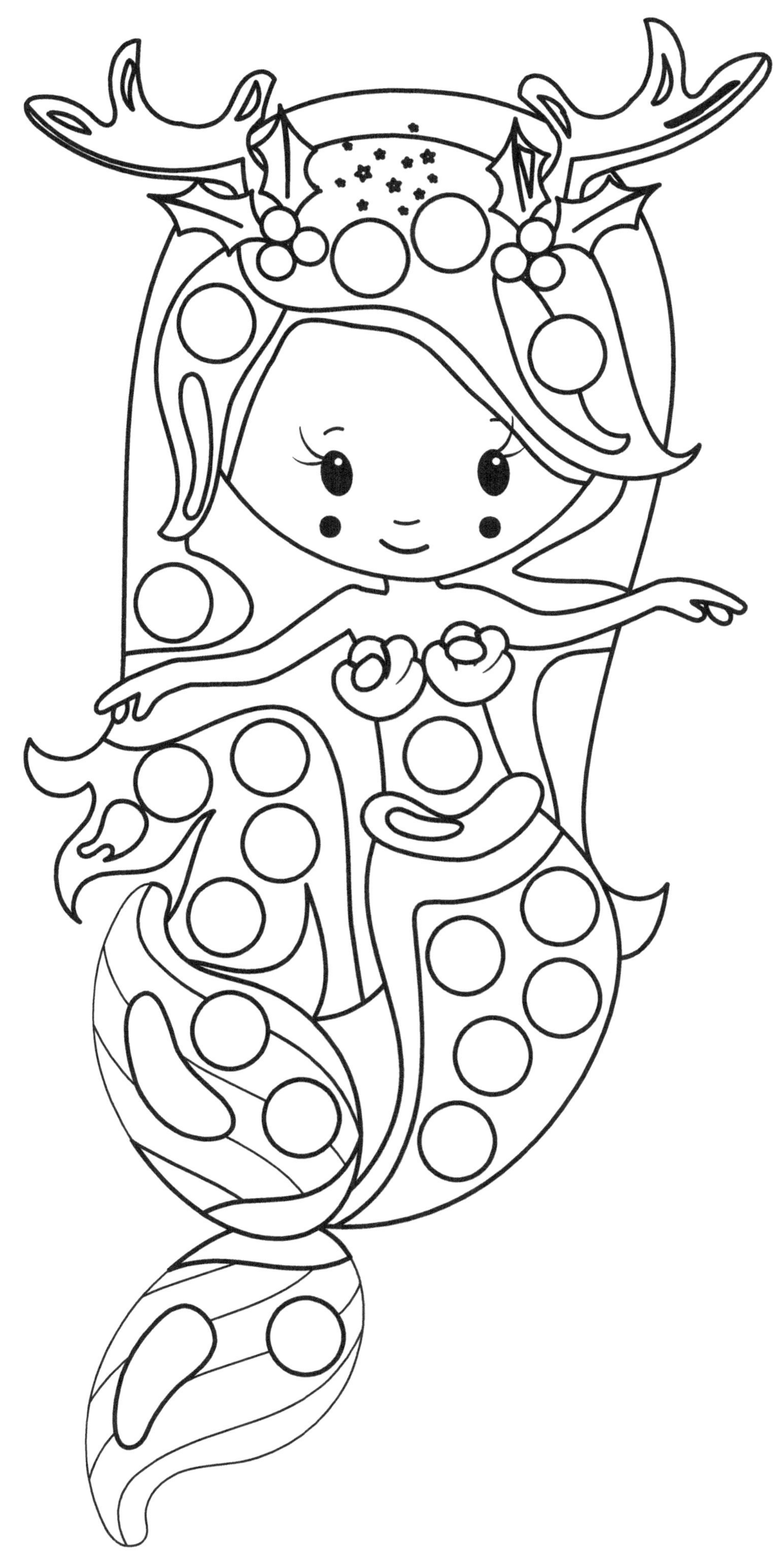

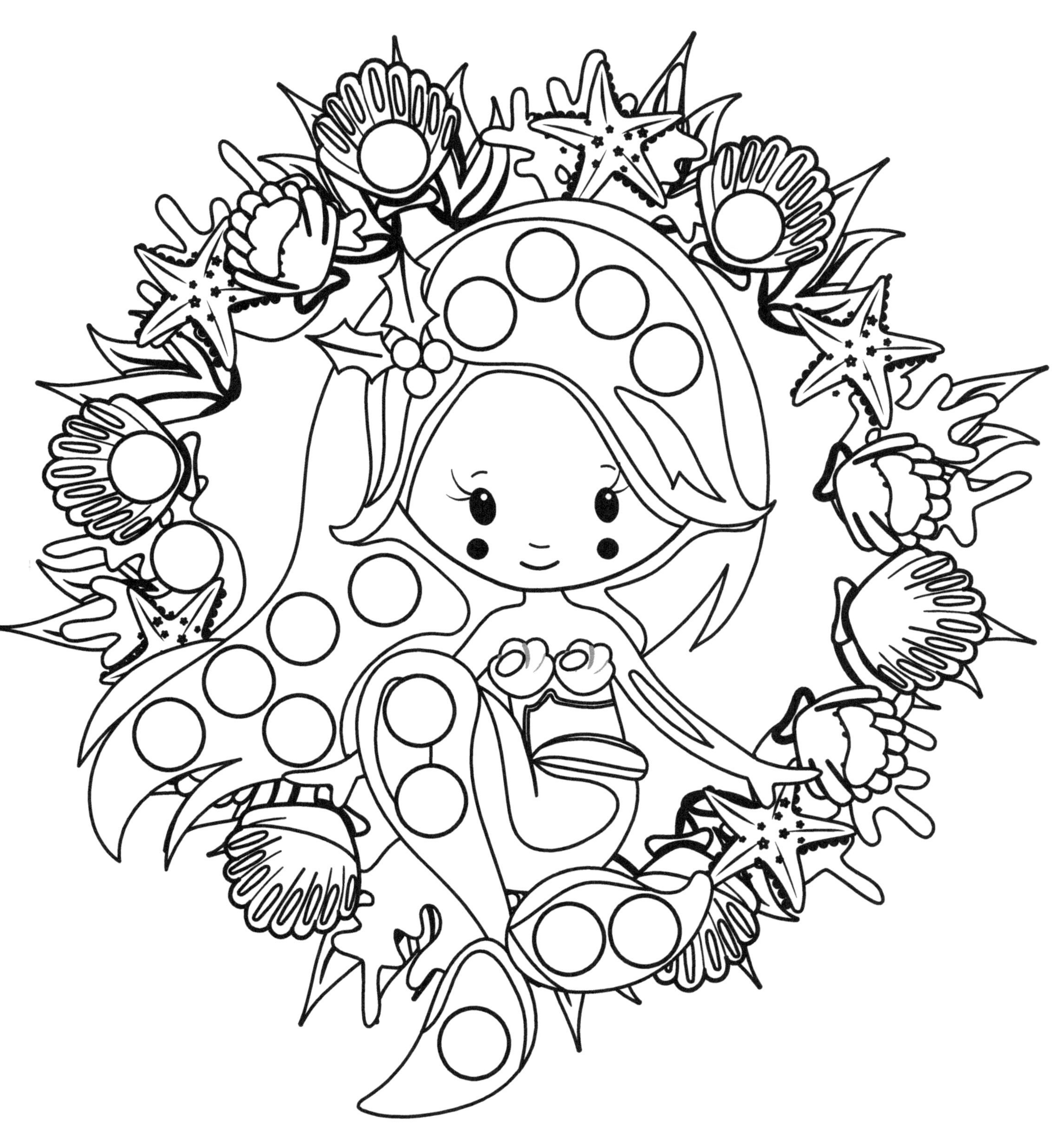

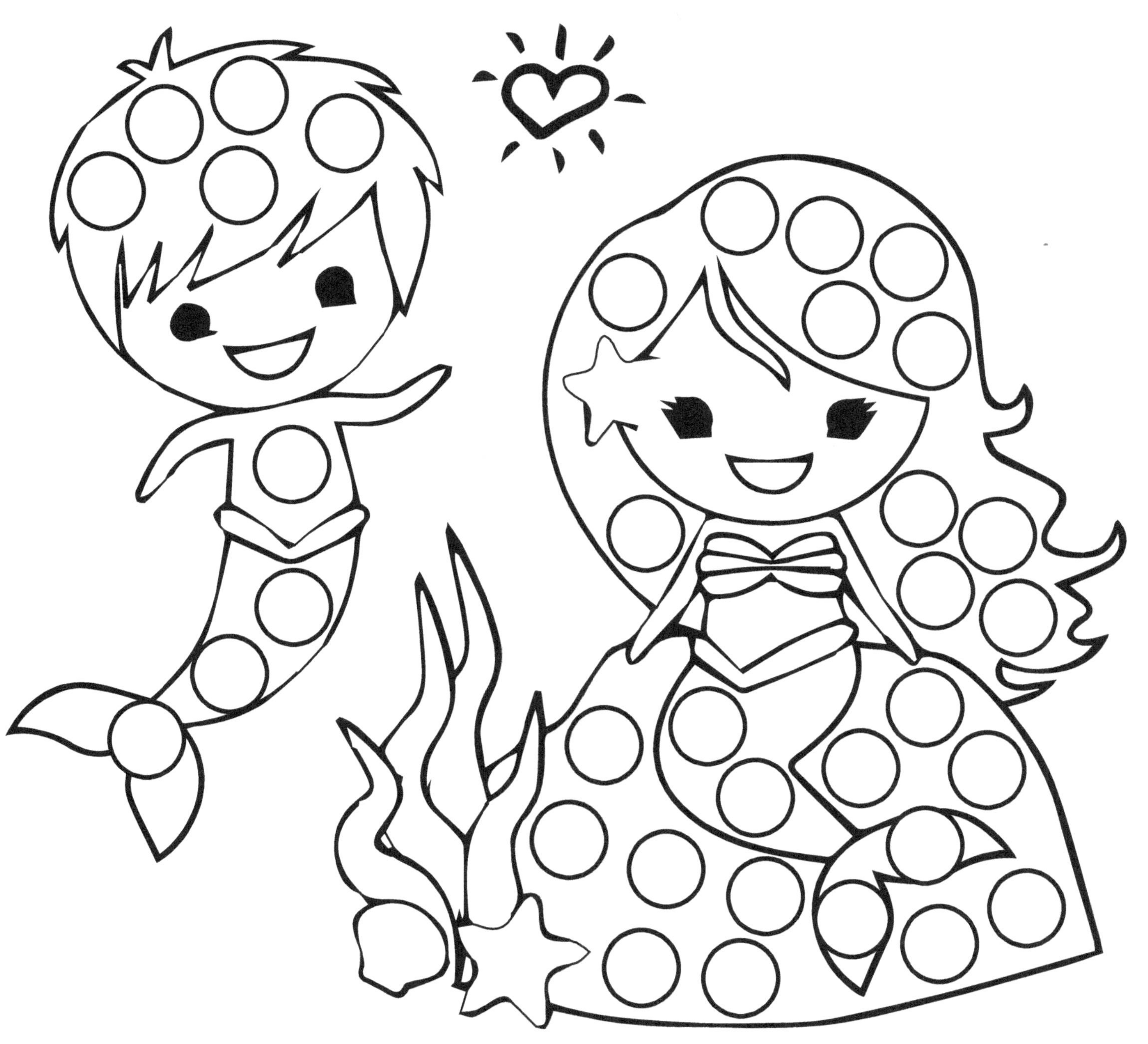

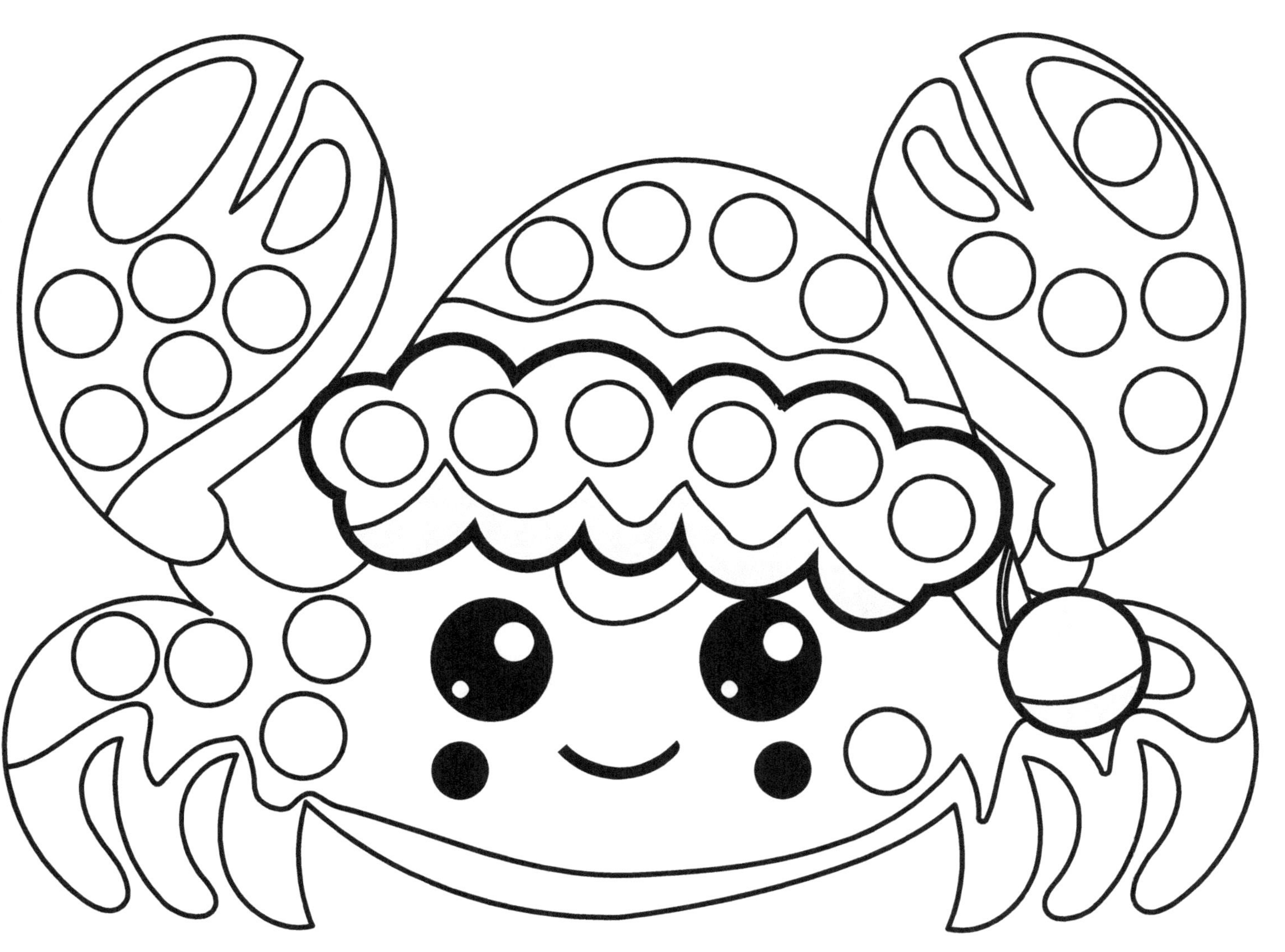

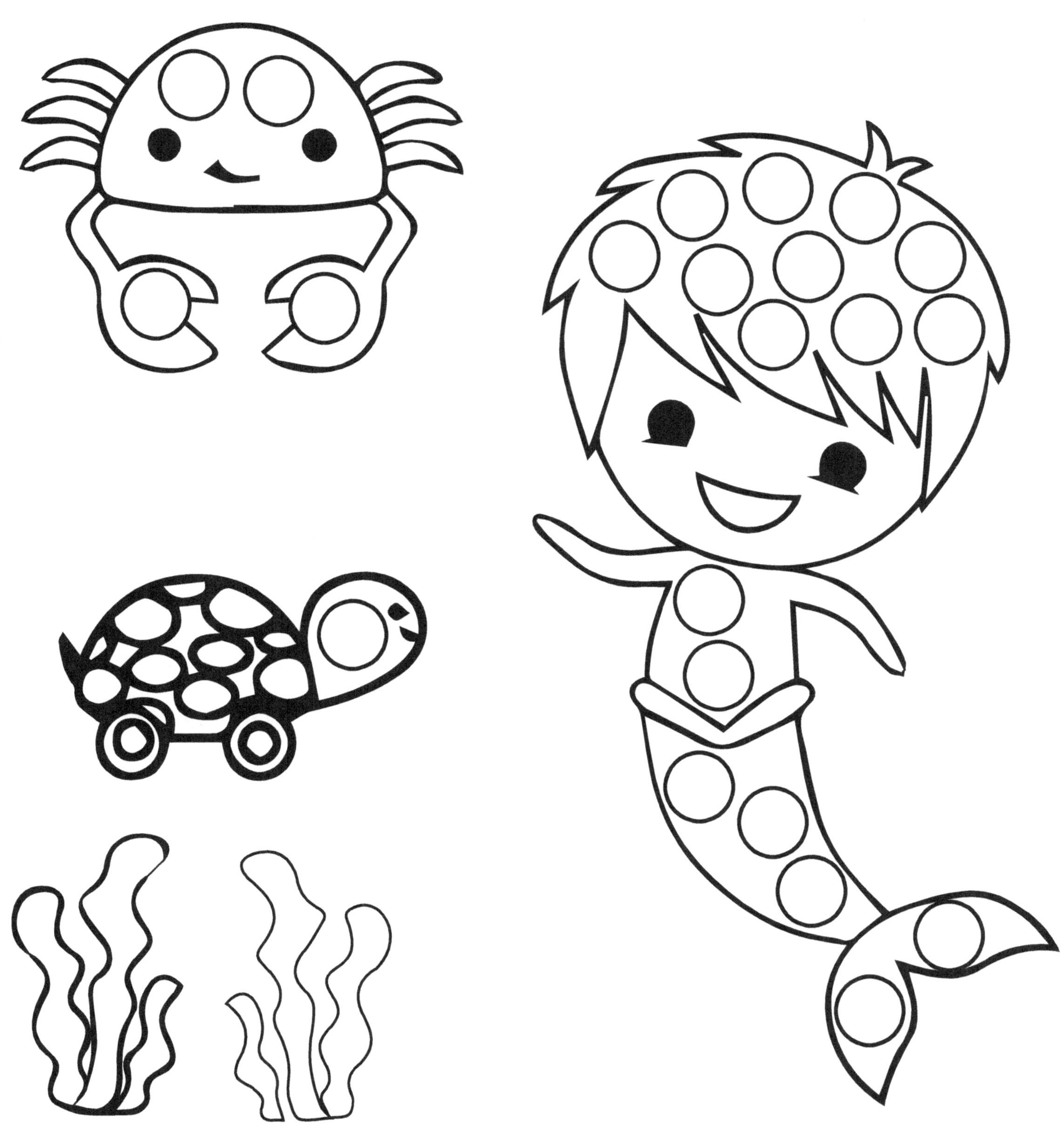

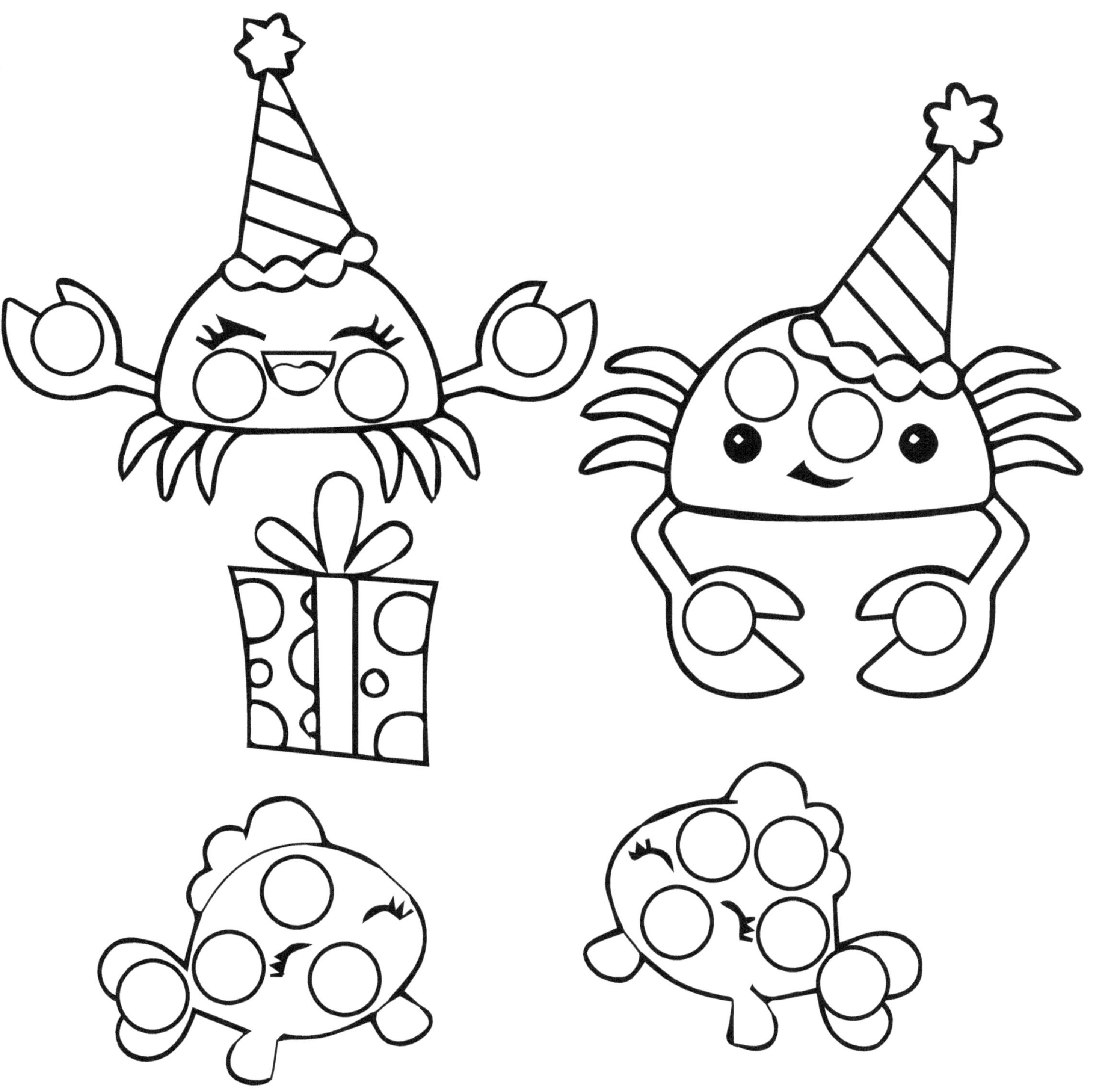

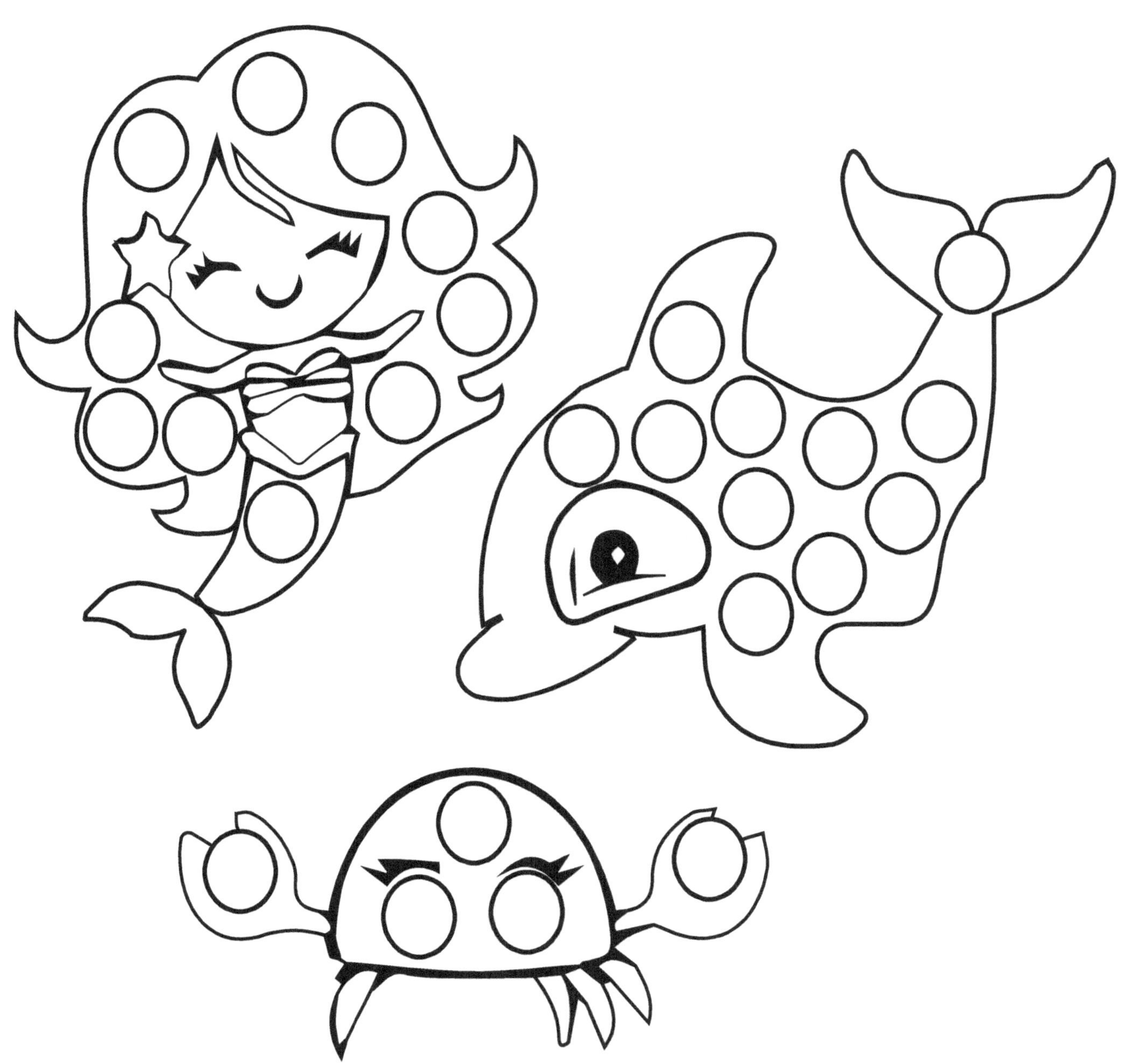

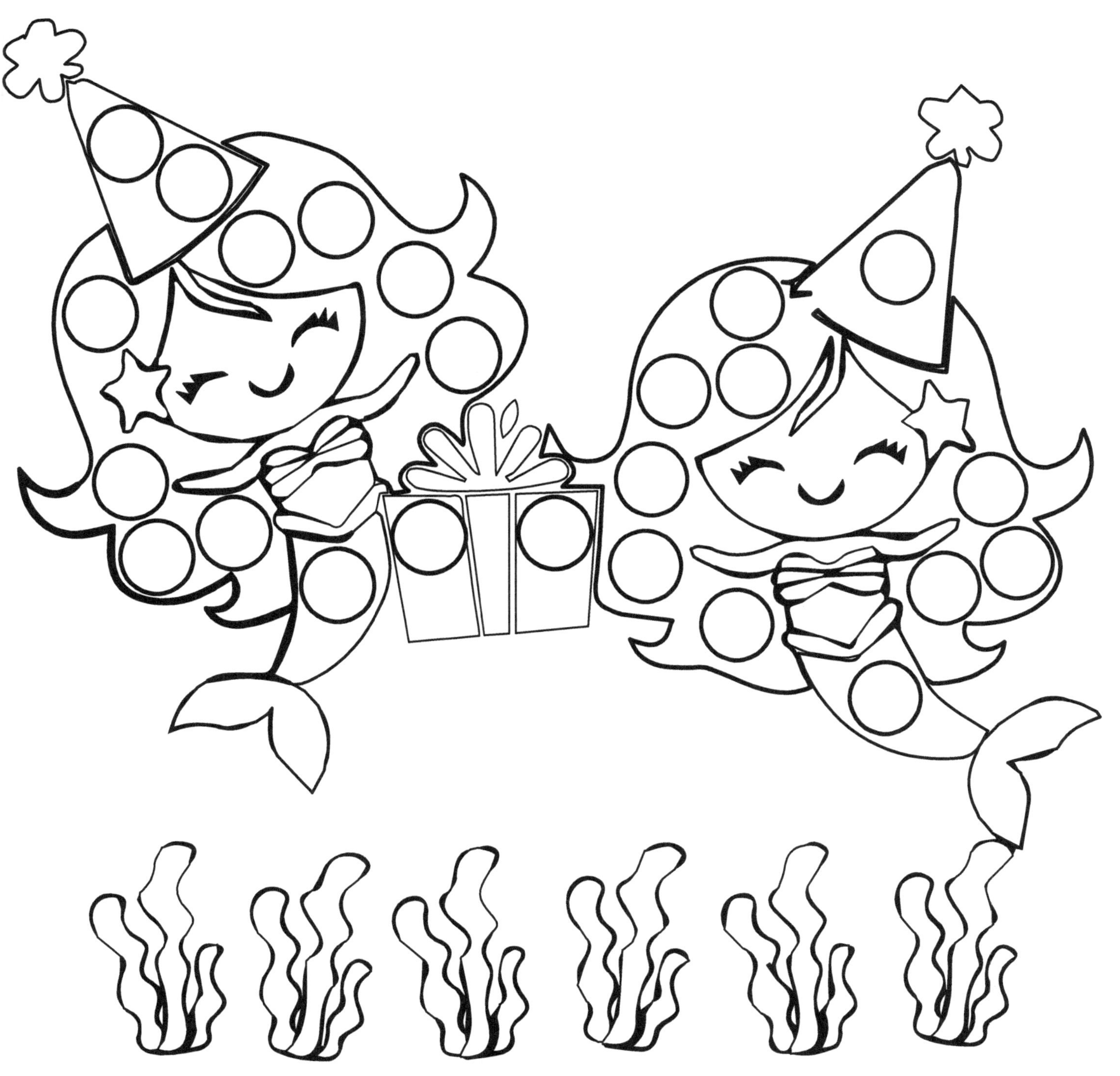

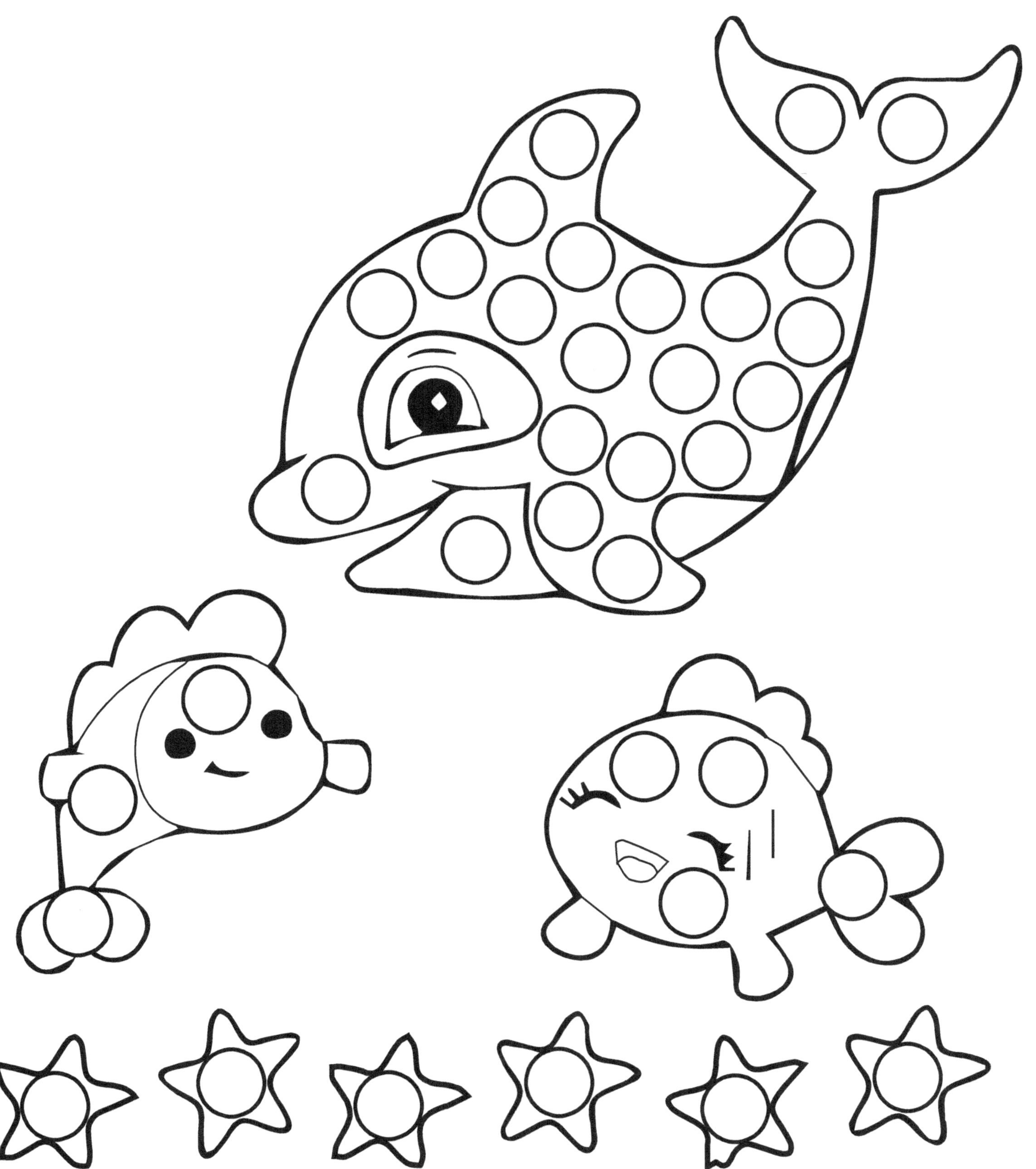

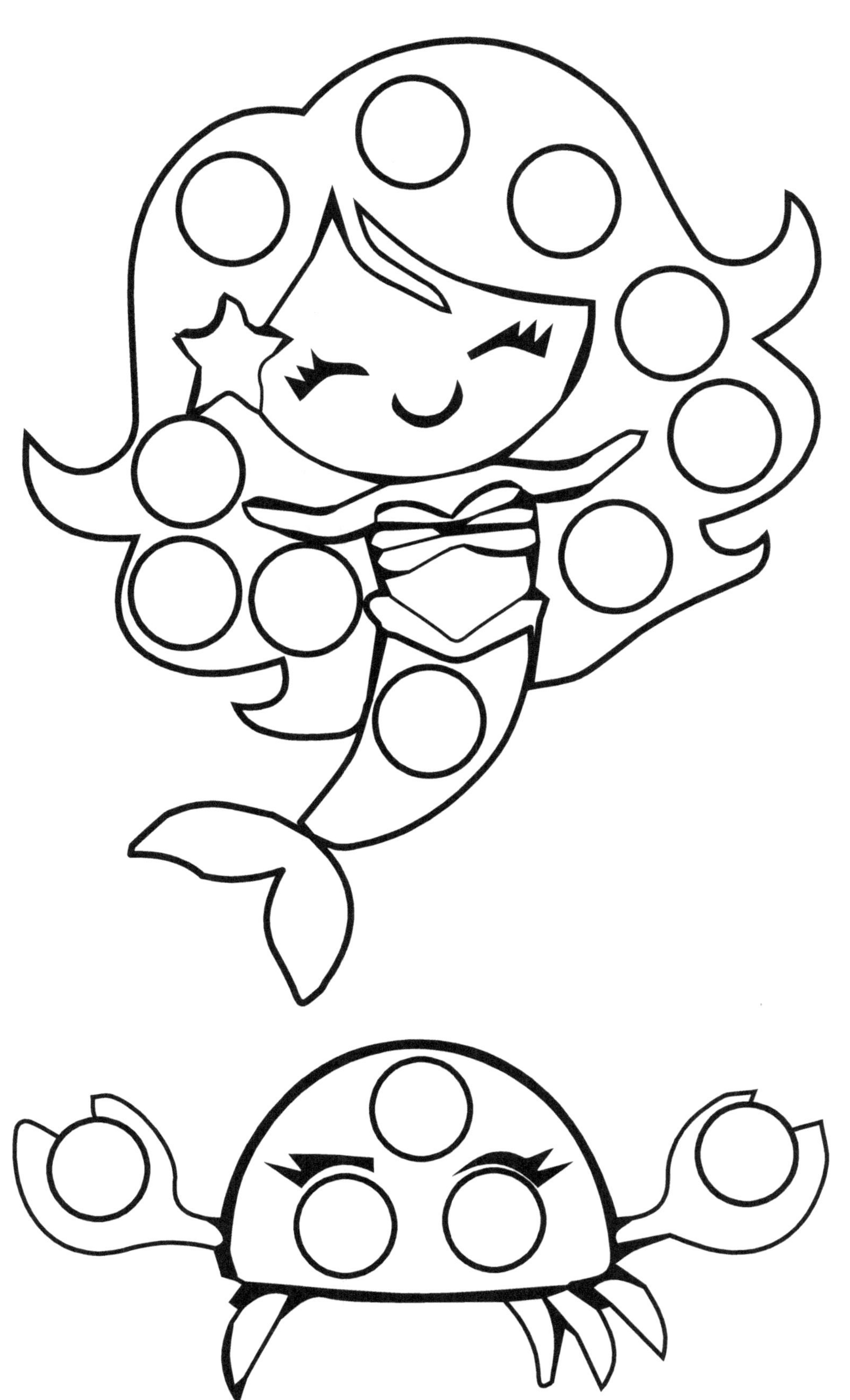

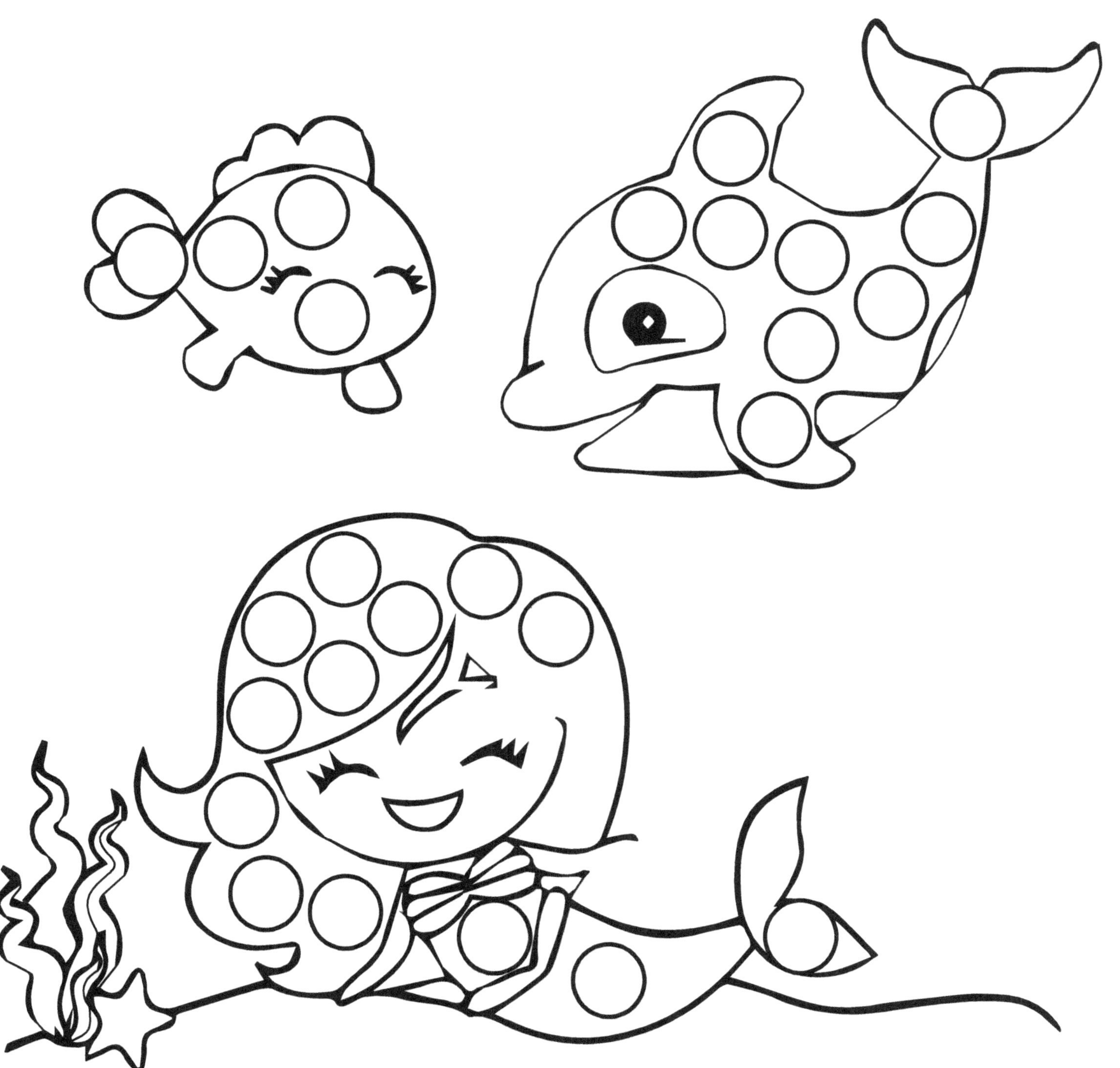

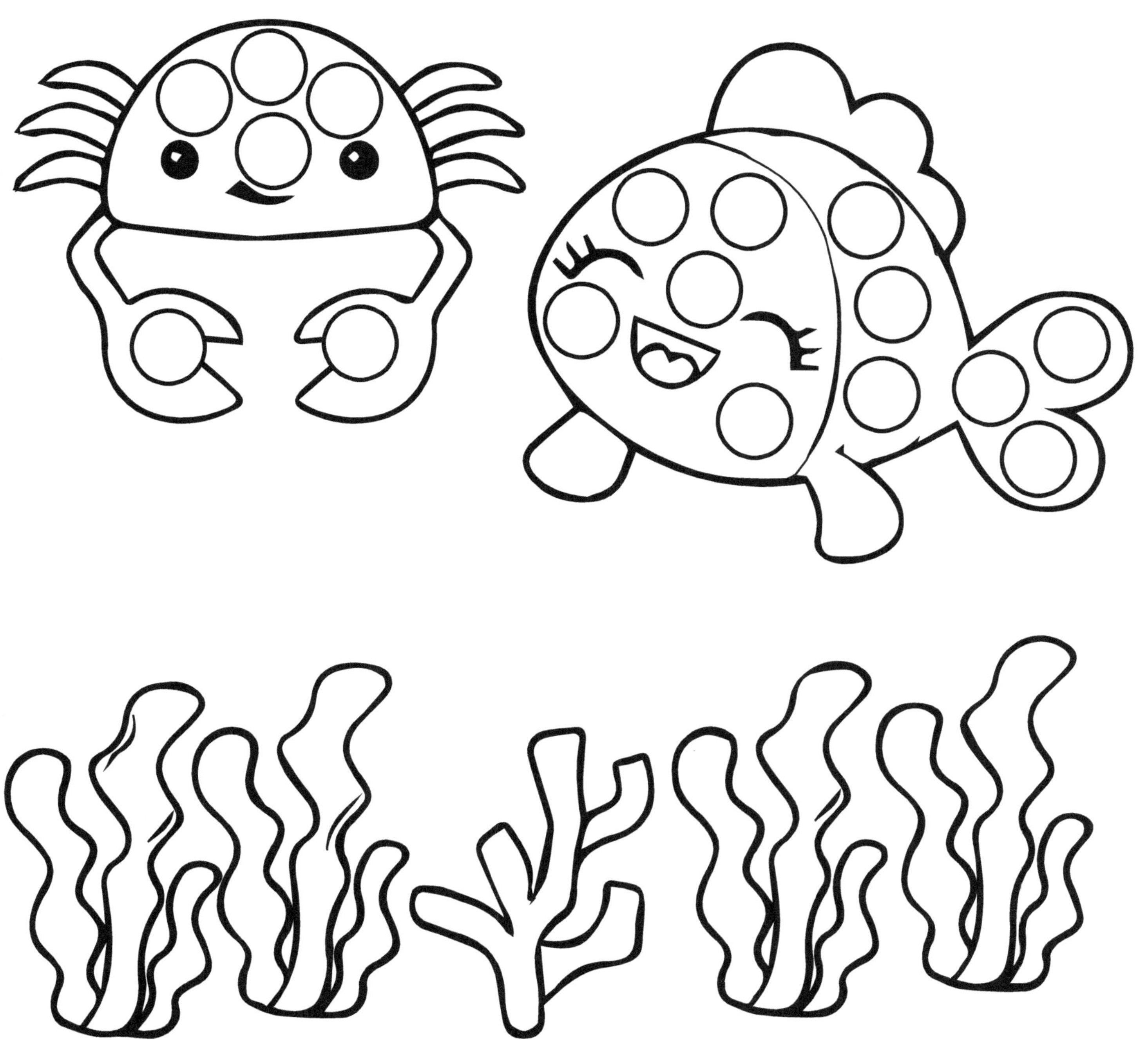

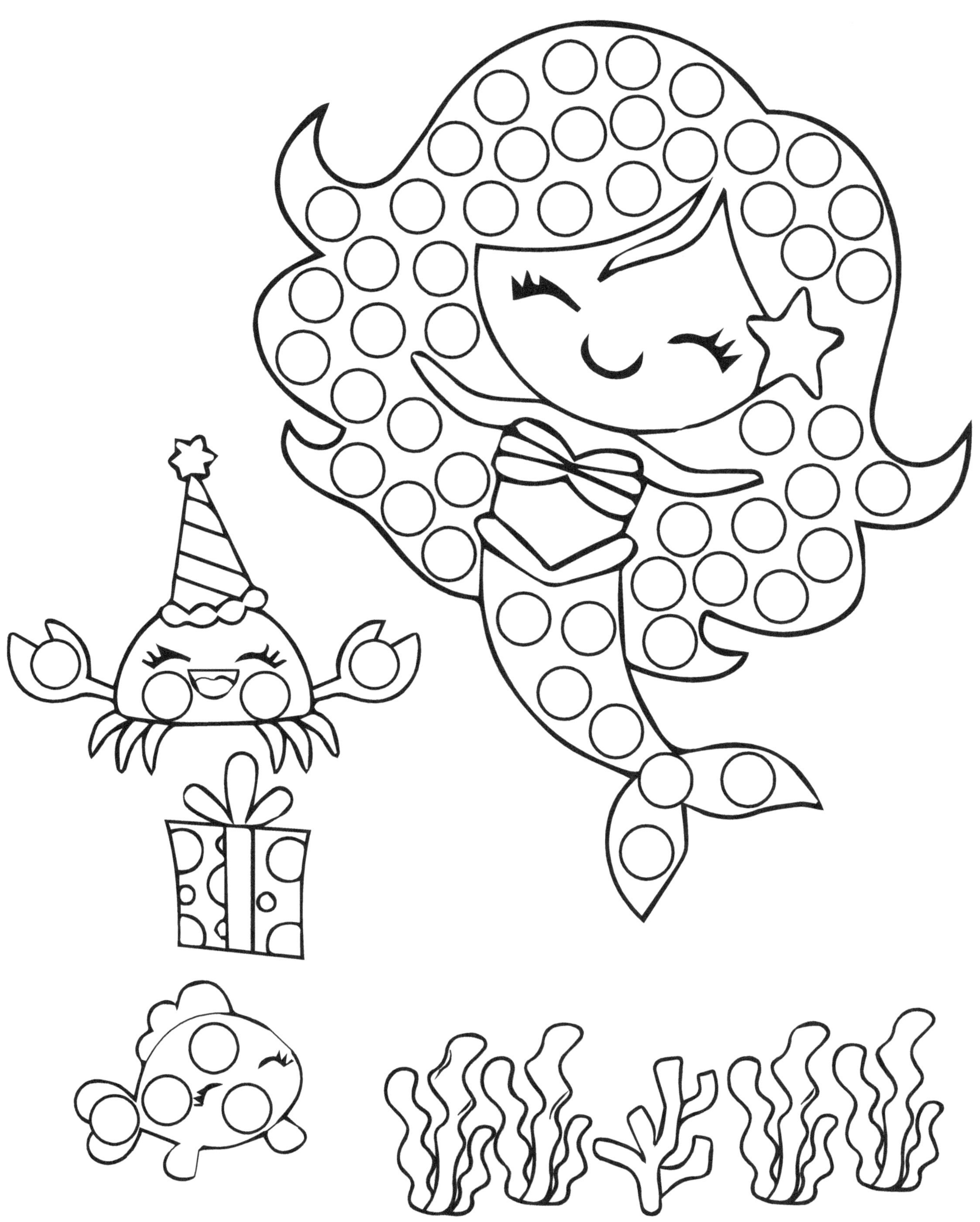

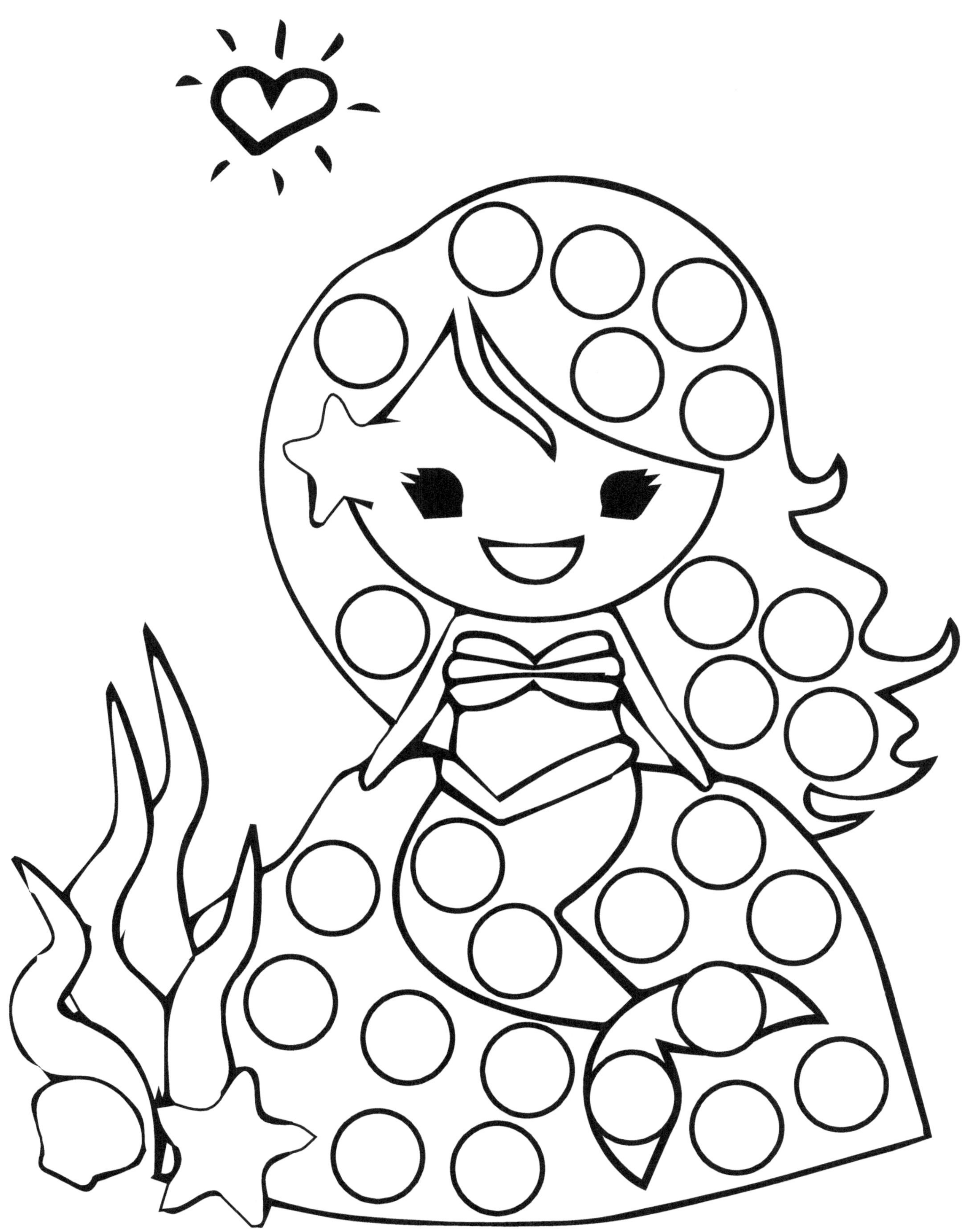

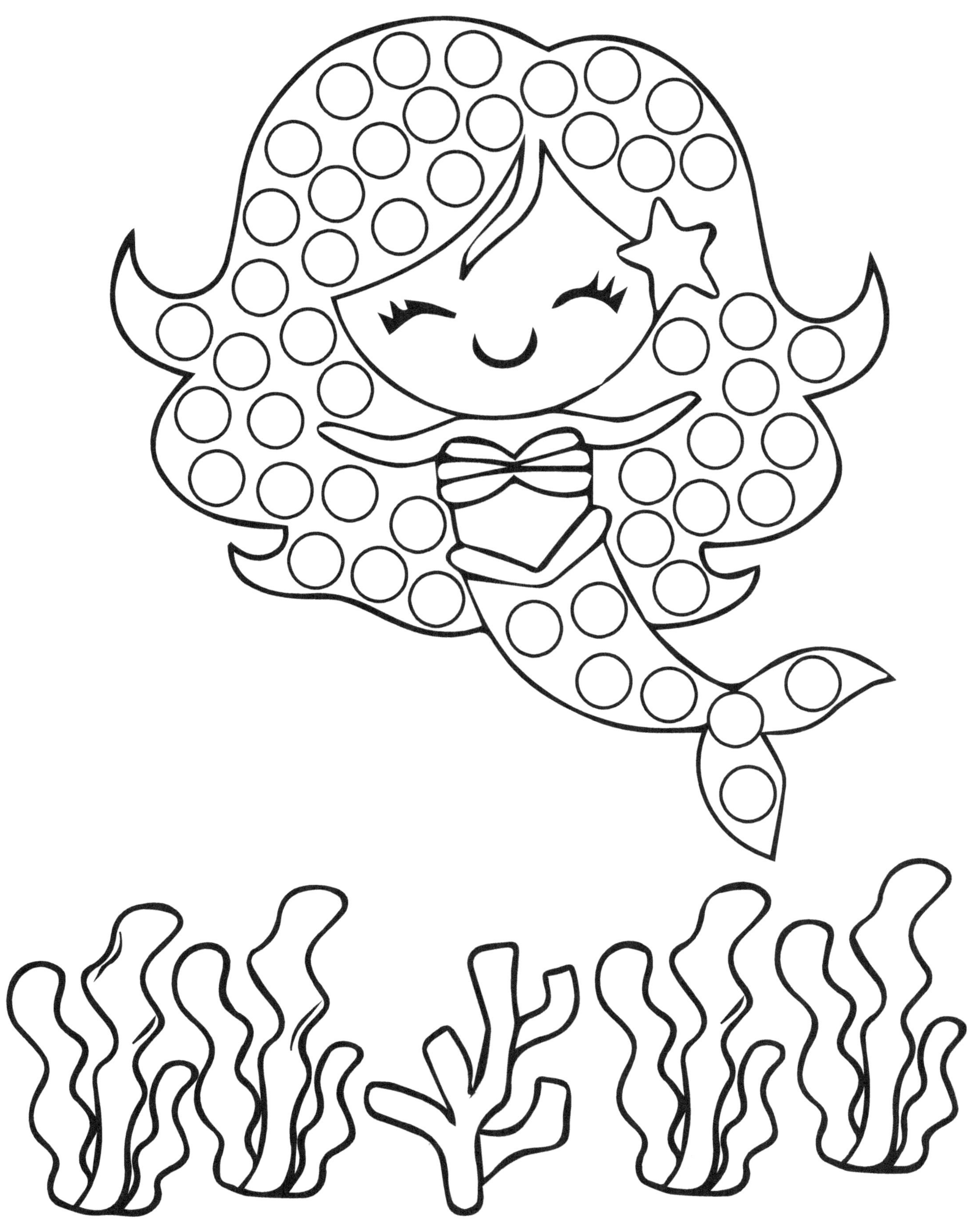

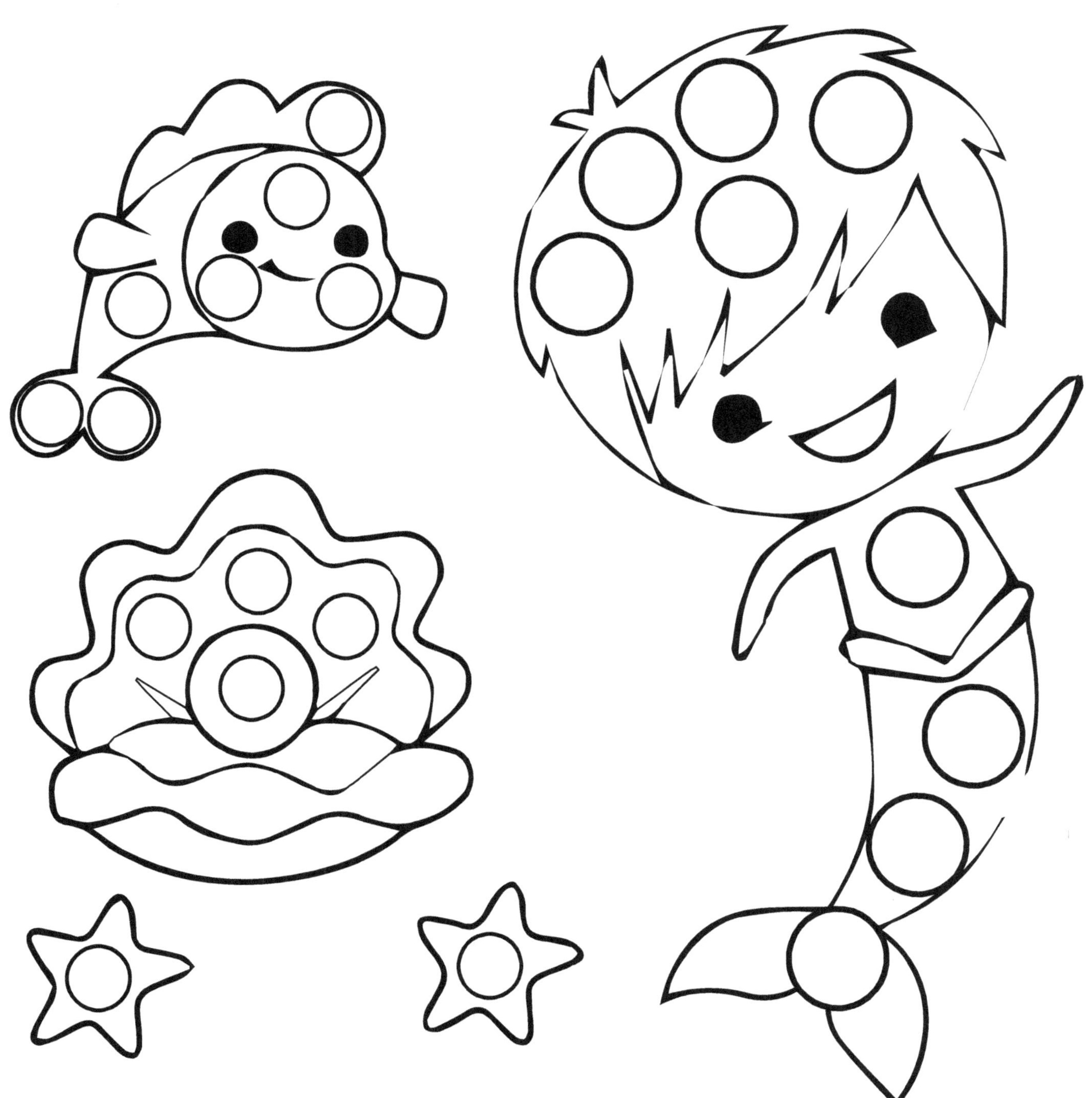

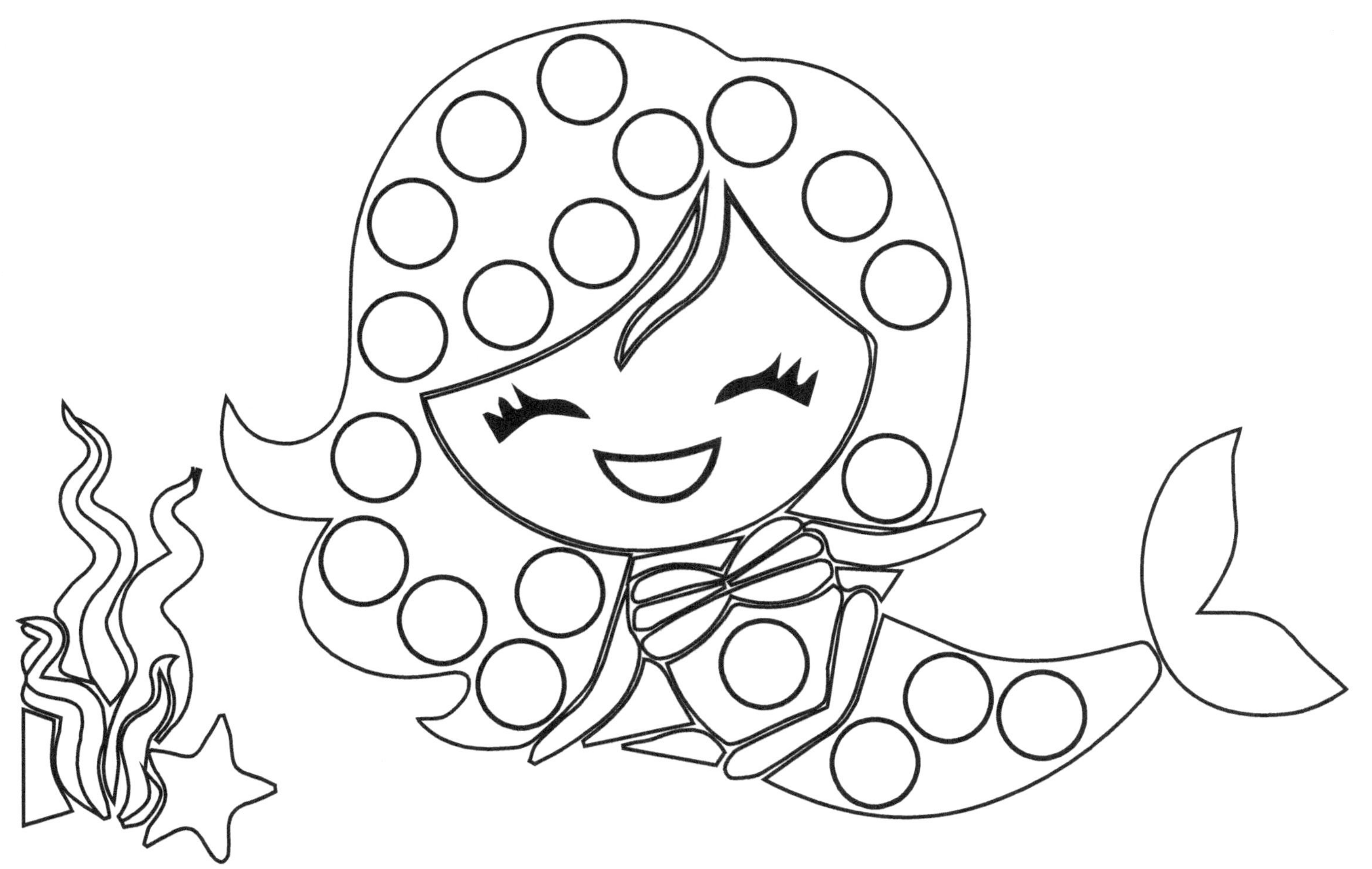

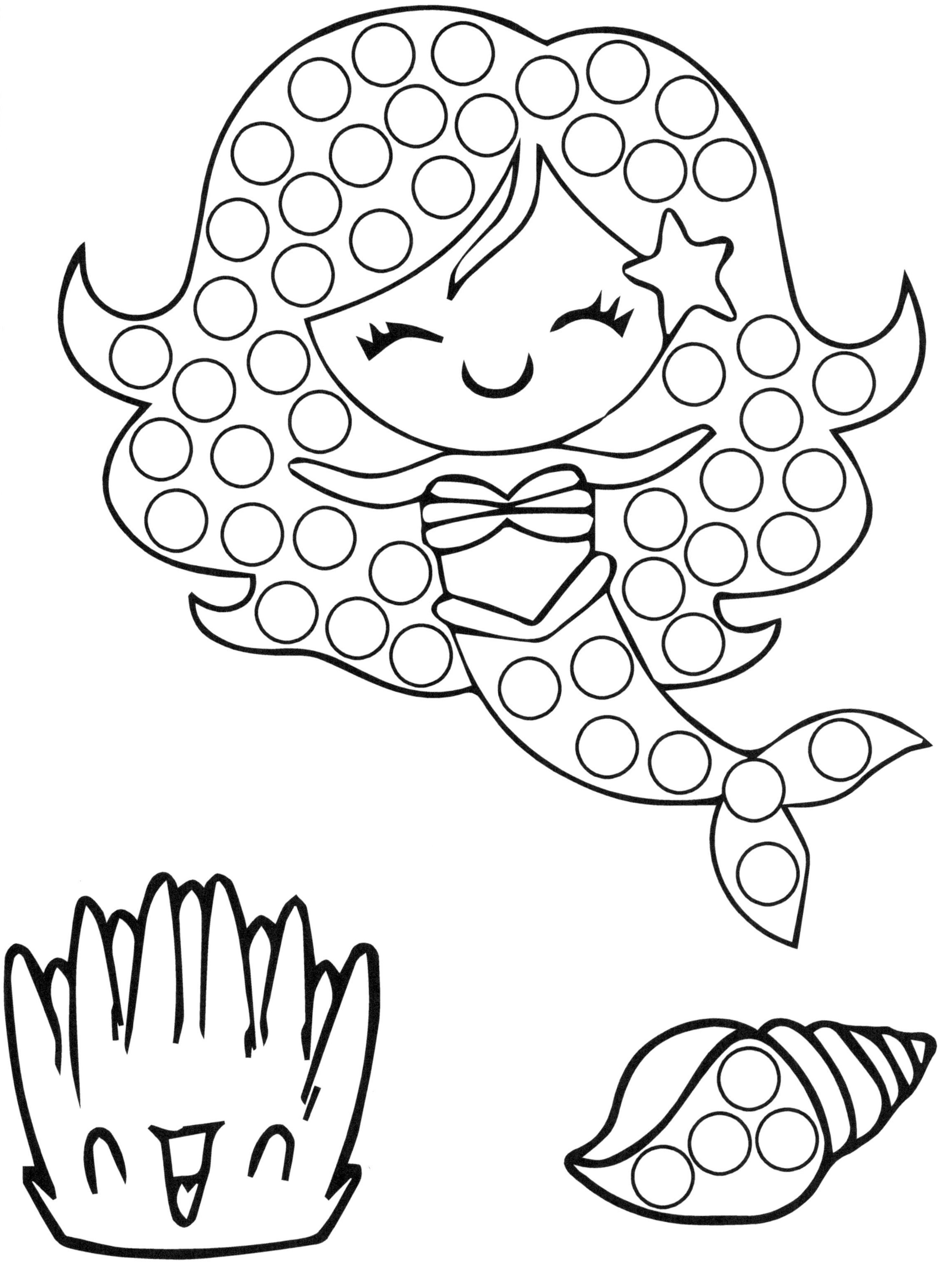

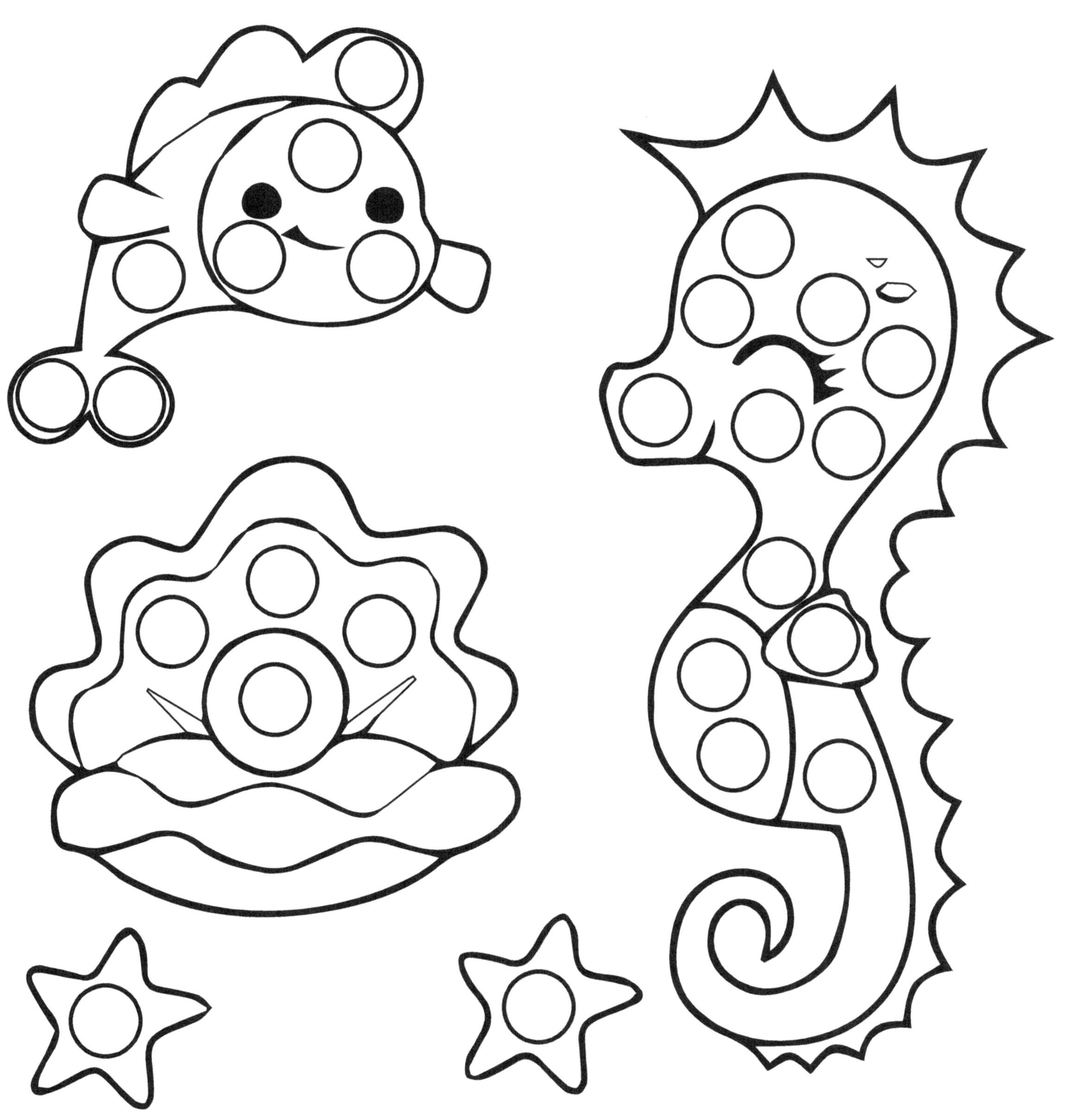

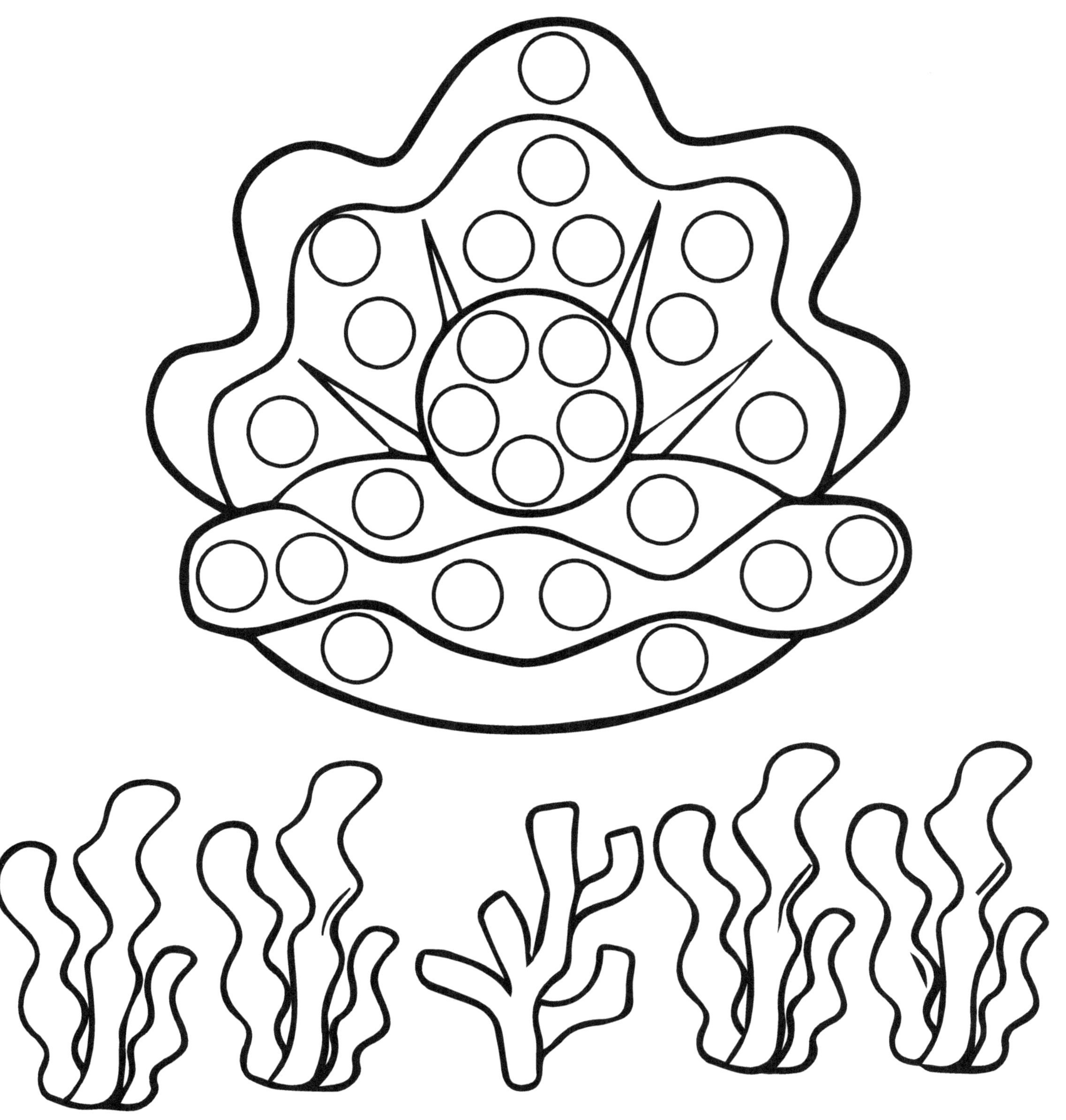

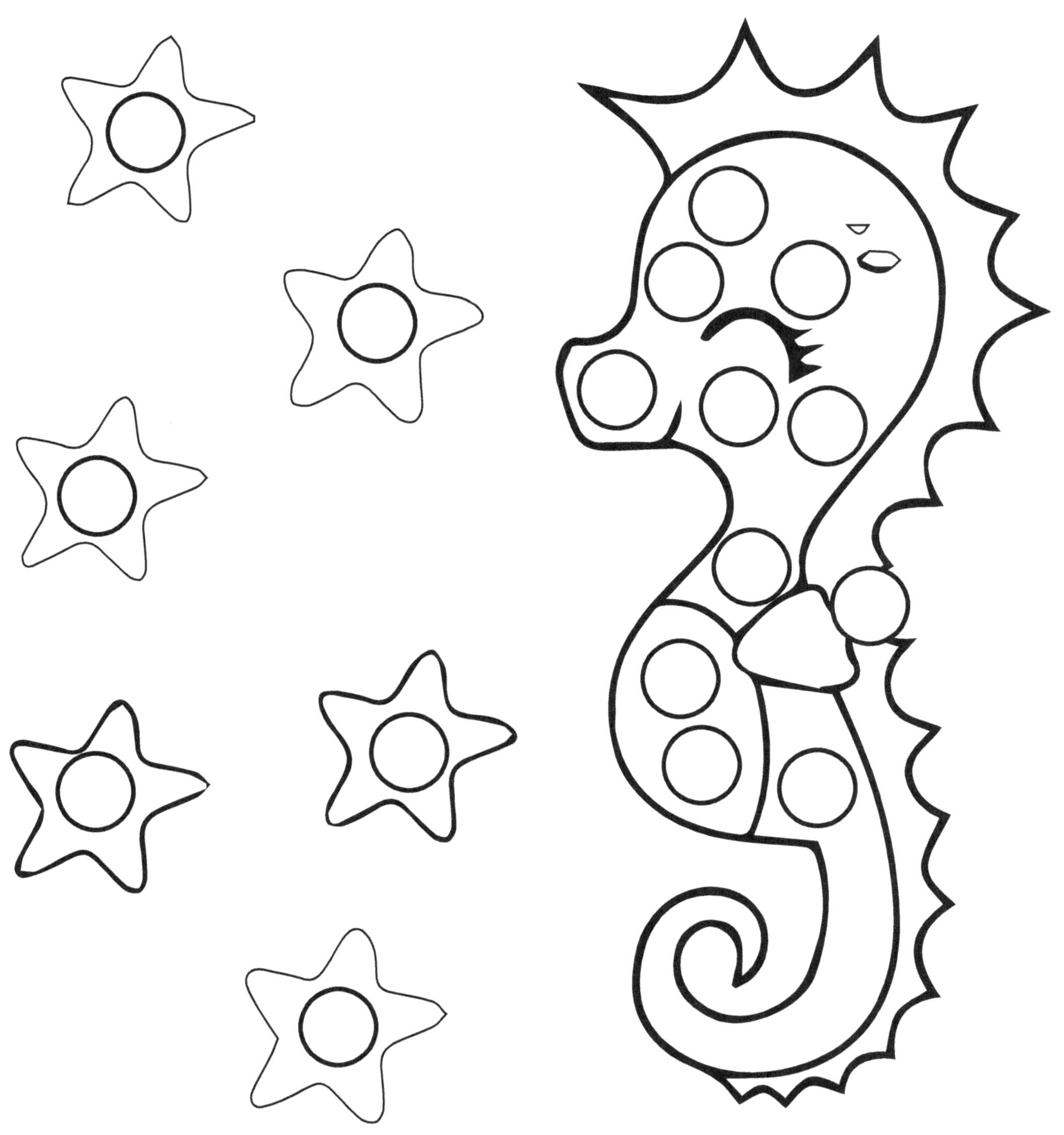

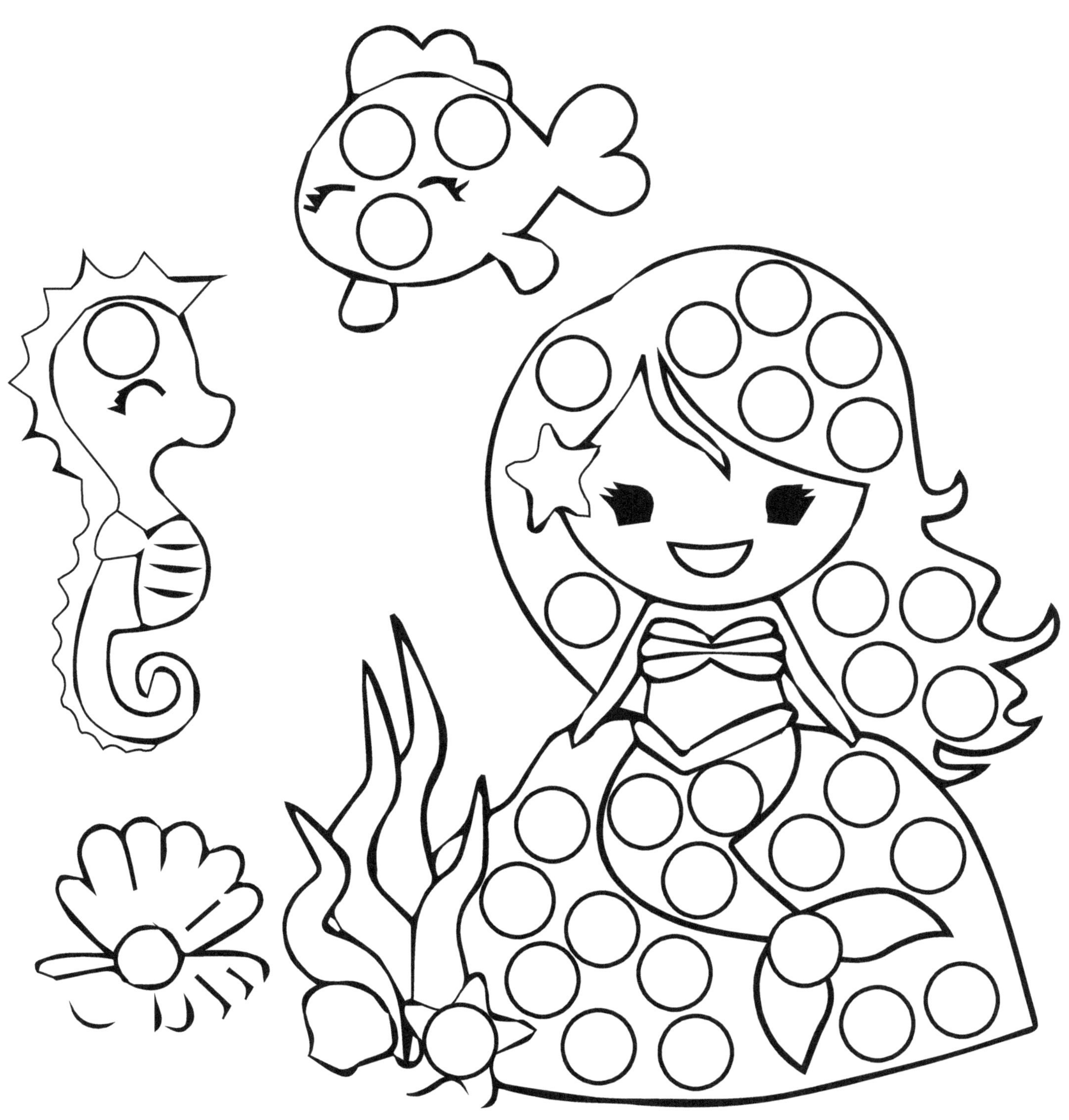